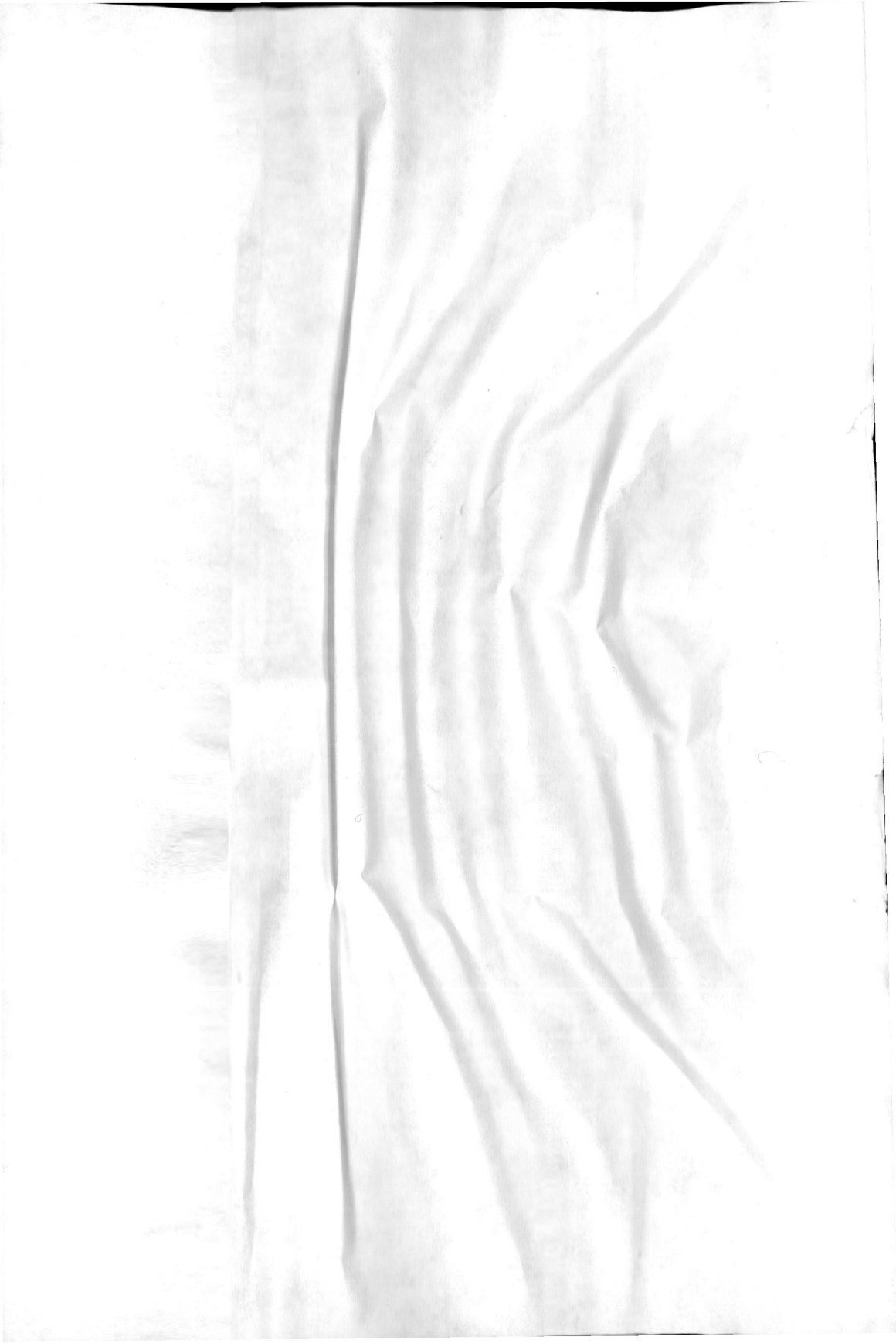

PHENOMENAL BUSINESS SUCCESS

PHENOMENAL
BUSINESS
SUCCESS

BREAKTHROUGH STRATEGIES
for MAXIMUM ACHIEVEMENT

SUCCESS
BOOKS®
Lake Mary, FL

CONTENTS

Foreword
By Robert A. Rohm, PhD 9

Preface
Phenomenal Business Success 13

CHAPTER 1
Living a Phenomenal Dream Life
From a Welfare Throwaway Kid to International
Business Coach
By Howard Partridge 17

CHAPTER 2
Built by Faith, Driven by Purpose
By Edwin Blosser 25

CHAPTER 3
From Breakdown to Breakthrough
Building a Life and Business That Matter
By Nathan Shafer 33

CHAPTER 4
Phenomenal Struggle Breeds Phenomenal Success
By Nick Nanton 43

CHAPTER 5
**The Pain and Pleasure of Submitting to
the Process of God's Perfect Plan**
By Michael Acerra 53

CHAPTER 6
Rock-Bottom Reboot
The Power of a Personal Audit
By Deanna Sullivan... 61

CHAPTER 7
It's Never Too Late
How Failure Forged My Future
By Michael Killen 71

CHAPTER 8
Crafting a Legacy Through Faith
By Nick and Jamie Hallas 79

CHAPTER 9
A Blueprint for the Making of a Leader
By Alyse Makarewicz 89

CHAPTER 10
You Rise
Leading Through the Storms of Change
By Cheri Perry 99

CHAPTER 11
Labels Aren't Limits
Mastering Success When the System Writes You Off
By Kevin Babb 109

CHAPTER 12
Battlefield to Boardroom
My Small-Business Fight for Survival
By Jim McDonough 119

FOREWORD

By Robert A. Rohm, PhD

Howard Partridge knows business! He learned it the hard way, from the School of Hard Knocks!

Howard started his business career several decades ago in LA (lower Alabama), working out of the trunk of his car. He didn't use the back seat of his car for work because that was his bedroom! You get the picture. And it was not a very pretty one. But he started, and that is often the hardest thing to do. Just get started. Anybody can complain and moan and groan about how difficult their circumstances are, but not everyone is willing to do something about them. Needless to say, Howard did not give up. He persevered until things started to turn around. Since he was already at the bottom of the barrel, he kept going until things had to get better. The only possible place he could go was up!

The best thing about Howard's situation was the fact that he was a learner. He began receiving on-the-job training while studying business success and the principles that helped others succeed. He started incorporating those same ideas, principles, and strategies into his own life and business—and what do you know, they worked! So in Howard's typical style, he began teaching and training other business owners on the same strategies that had worked for him. He didn't teach from theory. He taught from hands-on experience. Howard believed then, and believes now, that the best kind of learning comes from personal experience rather than theory. To Howard, life's most important lessons are best learned through experience, not just from a textbook or someone else's opinion.

In time Howard developed a group of devoted followers—people who wanted to be like him. He created a loyal following of aspiring entrepreneurs who were eager to follow his lead. Many of them may have lacked formal training, but all were willing to learn and grow through their own experience. Someone once wisely noted that you cannot export products you do not produce. These followers were learning from a master trainer—someone who could share proven principles he had tested and refined through hands-on work. Over time Howard became very successful. But the best part wasn't the money. It was the ability to help other people longing for a better, more rewarding, and more successful life. It's hard to say whether he found them or they found him. Either way, the law of attraction went to work, and they eventually found each other.

The book you now hold in your hands is the culmination of many years of mentoring, coaching, and training other aspiring business owners. Often people just need someone to guide them and help them see things differently, leading to a whole new way of life for them and their families. Inspiration and perspiration are a hard combination to beat.

The stories you are about to read are the result of hundreds of hours of hard work. They are the personal stories of people who have experienced real breakthroughs in their lives and businesses—stories of maximum achievement. And their stories aren't much different from yours, except these people have a burning desire to share them with others. I personally know many of the contributors to this book. I know firsthand about the struggles, challenges, fears, and tears they've encountered along their journeys. You will be greatly blessed and encouraged to take additional steps yourself toward becoming the person you were meant to be. Who knows, maybe you will be the next honors graduate from the School of Hard Knocks, which continues to produce winners and successful people every day.

To all the contributors of this book—congratulations! I am proud of you. I really am.

God bless you!

—**ROBERT A. ROHM, PhD**
PRESIDENT, PERSONALITY INSIGHTS INC.
ATLANTA, GEORGIA

PREFACE

Phenomenal Business Success

Every business owner starts their business with a dream. They start out with excitement and anticipation. They imagine all the trappings of a successful business—happy customers, lots of money, extravagant vacations, and let's not forget, the respect! Being your own boss, being a business owner, seems glamorous to others.

But after about three years of doing what you love, you realize that you not only have to do the work of the business, but you have to do the bookkeeping. You have to market your business. You have to sell; you have to do, well, everything!

Then you hire people. Now you not only have to deliver great service for your customer, but you have to manage other people. And for many business owners, that is the most frustrating part of all. In fact, many of them throw in the towel on having employees and sentence themselves to a lifetime of having to do everything themselves. They say goodbye to distraction-free dinner with the family. They say goodbye to spending time with their kids. They say goodbye to the dream they had of going on luxurious vacations.

The problem is that most business owners are never properly trained in the business disciplines such as leadership, marketing, sales, systems, and administration. You might be the best at delivering your product or service. But you find out that you are woefully unprepared for the business parts, especially managing others!

You need a breakthrough, a breakthrough for maximum achievement that will help you realize your business dream.

This book is designed to help you do exactly that. I am grateful for this book project and quite proud, as all of the coauthors are business-coaching clients of mine.

As you read their stories of phenomenal business success, you will find that they faced the same kinds of situations that you may have experienced. Instead of staying stuck, they broke through and achieved maximum achievement in their respective industries.

Here's a breakdown of the title of this book and what I hope will become true for you.

Phenomenal means very remarkable, extraordinary. You can be that. Your business can be that.

Business—America was built by entrepreneurs, and small business is the backbone of America and perhaps the only institution that's keeping everything together. It can be a phenomenal experience that brings you wealth, prestige, and freedom, or it can be a brutal taskmaster. The choice is yours.

Success—The one and only reason your business exists is to be a vehicle to help you achieve your life goals. *Success* means that your business works for you, delivering the life you really want. First, set your life goals; then, build systems, develop yourself as a leader, and build that phenomenal dream team that you will need to reach your biggest dreams.

Breakthrough—You will notice in my story as well as all the others that our biggest breakthroughs came in the form of a coach. A coach can take you to levels you will never reach on your own. Just ask Michael Jordan, or anyone else who has achieved a phenomenal level of success.

Strategies for maximum achievement—Every business owner has strategies, whether they realize it or not. The problem is that their strategies haven't been evaluated to determine whether they are the best strategies.

The goal is not to do your best but to do things the best they can be done. Tweak your strategies until they work consistently, and then put them into a system. The right systems will give you maximum achievement and will help you become phenomenally successful.

Every phenomenally successful business requires phenomenal systems, phenomenal leadership, and a phenomenal dream team. If you have a dream but no team, you have to give up the dream or build up the team.

Finally, as I mentioned, our breakthroughs came through coaching. The number one reason business owners don't grow or do as well as they could is what I call FTI (failure to implement).

Therefore, all the coauthors of this book did just two things:

1. They learned the proven systems.

2. They implemented them.

As a result, they got the breakthrough they needed and are now leading phenomenally successful businesses and lives.

CHAPTER 1

LIVING A PHENOMENAL DREAM LIFE

*From a Welfare Throwaway Kid to
International Business Coach*

By Howard Partridge

I like to tell people that I'm from LA. Of course they assume I mean Los Angeles, and either they cross their arms, sensing a bit of arrogance, or their eyebrows go up with an expression that says, "Cool." Then, I reveal that I am from lower Alabama. I love that little schtick!

I grew up on welfare in Mobile, Alabama, with seven kids crammed into a six-hundred-square-foot shack. The roof on that house was so bad that we had to get out all the pots and pans to catch the leaks. My mother fed us on a hundred dollars a month from the welfare department.

Two months before my eighteenth birthday, I got kicked out of the house by my stepdad. I deserved it. I was a wild kid. The problem is that I had *no money.*

I scraped up enough for a Greyhound bus to Houston, Texas. When I stepped off that bus, I had twenty-five cents in my pocket. I became a waiter and worked in really high-end restaurants, where I wore a tuxedo and flamed dishes at the table. Setting stuff on fire inside at that age was pretty cool, but I always wanted my own business.

At that time, I was just making enough money to pay the rent. Then, I met my wife, Denise Concetta Antionette Pennella. Now that's Italian! She was from New Jersey. And where am I from? Lower Alabama. Oh boy, this is gonna be a good match!

We went to New Jersey to get married, and when you marry into an Italian family, you don't get wedding presents; you get *cash*. We got three thousand dollars in wedding money. There was a friend of the family who was the same age as me, twenty-three at the time, but this guy was driving around in a shiny red Mercedes convertible. I thought, "I want to know what he does, and I want to know if it's legal!"

As it turned out, he owned his own business. As soon as I got home from our honeymoon, I spent the entire three thousand dollars starting my first business out of the trunk of my car.

It was exciting. I had respect. I loved serving my customers. But after about thirteen years in business I found myself working twenty-four hours a day, seven days a week. I felt like a slave to my business. I made good money, but I had no life.

Can you relate?

It was then that my first breakthrough came.

People loved our service, which meant I had lots of prospects. But I couldn't get to all the people who wanted to give me money. My small team didn't know how to sell my service, and no one could make a move without me micromanaging their every move because I had no systems.

One hot August day in Houston, as I was running back and forth between my warehouse and my office, overseeing the repair of a machine and trying to return calls, sweat dripping off my face onto the stack of papers on my desk, my mentor walked in for our weekly meeting.

Bill Beckham was one of my pastors. A tall, green-eyed east Texas man with white hair and a perfectly trimmed white beard noticed the chaos and spoke in his Southern drawl: "Howard, you need *The E-Myth*." "What is an e-myth?" I thought. I got Michael E. Gerber's book, *The E-Myth Revisited* and devoured it.

I realized that I needed systems, and I saw that not only could I get my business more organized with systems, but eventually I could have a turnkey business, a business that I didn't have to work in!

If you've ever heard the tip "Work *on* the business instead of in it," let me set the record straight: Michael E. Gerber, the man *Inc.* magazine called the world's number one small-business guru, coined it.

As it turns out, that book changed my business and changed my life. What's more is after I started my business coaching and training business, I found myself sharing the stage with Michael. I've hired him to speak at my own conferences, and not only have we shared the stage together many times, but he became a friend. Oddly enough, a couple of years ago, after living his entire eighty-six years in California, he moved to the Houston area.

Michael lives less than thirty minutes from me and is the reason you are holding this book in your hand. Celebrity Branding did a coauthored book with Michael, and my brother was one of the authors. He told me he was coming to Houston for a special dinner with Michael, Nick Nanton, and the other coauthors of that book.

My brother was allowed to bring someone to the dinner, so I hired a driver with a black SUV to drive my brother, Michael Gerber, and his family to the dinner. I made sure I was sitting next to Nick. That was the genesis of this book.

Reading (and acting upon) *The E-Myth Revisited* was a huge breakthrough for me. I brought on a couple of industry friends as partners, and we began the process of building systems in that first business. I was in charge of marketing and sales, one partner was in charge of operations, and the other was in charge of administration.

But another challenge was afoot.

When we first started together, there was a lot of excitement. My marketing worked! We had lots of business coming in. I created a sales process that anyone could follow and close the sale. But as the sales rose, so did the debt.

As the debt piled up, the tension between the partners rose as well. After eight years one of my partners resigned and requested a buyout (on payments, of course), which I quickly agreed to, just to get rid of the arguments and frustration. My other partner and I immediately began to disagree about how to move forward. Our partnership ended after a heated argument. I gave him the same buyout terms as my first partner.

Now I was down two main players, the pile of debt was staring me down, and the loan payments to my partners were the same amount as their previous salary! This wasn't even a lateral move! Plus, I had to hire a general manager to look after things when I wasn't there! Now I have more money going out! The business was surviving on high-interest credit cards. Our line of credit stayed maxed out. My partners would be paid off in five years, and my sales and marketing skills were strong. I sensed I could pull the business out of the debt spiral, but the interest on my loans was so high I could never catch up. No banker in their right mind would touch me.

But another breakthrough was about to come.

Enter Wonder Woman Ellen Rohr. Ellen was a financial consultant who had a financial system I could follow. I decided to buy Ellen's package (on a high-interest credit card, of course). My back was against the wall, and the only choice I had was to figure out the finances, or fire my general manager and manage the business myself, which was doing north of two million per year at this time.

I sure didn't want to manage the company all by myself, so I shared Ellen's package with my manager and the bookkeeper, who was his daughter. But they didn't implement the program. So I paid even more money to bring Ellen in to show them how to use it.

After reviewing everything, she gave us a plan to pull out of the debt. We had to raise our prices, and we put a compensation plan in place that would reward the right behaviors. Great! Now I could see the light. She helped us create a budget to follow that spelled out the numbers.

Breakthrough! I could now see how following Ellen's system,

we would be profitable, and I wouldn't have to lose sleep over the stress of paying bills.

But then something happened.

After Ellen left town, my manager failed to use the system! And he didn't require the bookkeeper to use it either! Now I was beyond frustrated. I was angry. We had a leadership problem. I ended up letting both of them go on the same day. That was not fun. I restructured the company and put the right people in the right positions. I began to practice better leadership.

Along the way, I was not a good leader. I would show up at the office and bark out orders, pointing out the things that were out of place, done wrong, not getting done. I was intense. One morning one of my employees tapped on my door and asked if she could see me for a moment. She explained how scary I was when I marched through the office and that there were living, breathing human beings there and that it might do me good to at least say hello to them.

Another breakthrough came.

I began to learn leadership from Rick Jones, who had been with Dale Carnegie for thirty-three years and owned the Houston franchise for twenty years (which was the number one franchise in the world). He mentored me on leadership, and I began to learn from John Maxwell and others.

I had no idea that later on Rick would become a coach on my team and become like a father to me. And I had no idea that I would be personally mentored by John Maxwell and become his very first certified coach.

I met with my new team every month to mentor them and to focus on how we would have a record month each and every month, which we did. Getting the right team in place was key to me getting free. Now we were profitable, I had a great team in place, and I was *turnkey*! Today, that business does four million per year without paid advertising and is super profitable. And I don't have to be there. Ever.

When I got my business turnkey, my colleagues noticed. I was part of a small association and began to share some of my systems with that group. They liked what I had to share, so I began training business owners on my systems.

Over the next ten years, I became a slave to that business too! I was doing all the marketing, all the sales, all the coaching, and all the teaching. Thank God I had someone to do the accounting. I never got into debt with that business.

I found myself thinking about quitting. I was in Clearwater, Florida, when my next breakthrough came. I was frustrated because I saw other people in the coaching/training space who seemed to be extremely successful, but I didn't feel successful like them. Again, I was making good money, but I felt stuck. A lot of my promotions weren't working.

Walking along the beach, I was talking out loud to myself: "I've got to find someone who has been where I want to go, or has worked with someone who has been where I want to go."

My phone rang.

It was Mark Ehrlich. I met Mark through Michael Gerber. As Mark and I reconnected, I began to sense that he might be able to help me. I asked him to audit my workshop, which he did. The result? I did everything wrong, according to him. Over breakfast the next morning, he asked me about my vision. The more I shared, the more excited he became.

"Can you help me?" I said. When he told me how much it would be to meet with him over the phone weekly, I gulped. But I knew that I was spinning my wheels, so I agreed.

One of the first things Mark had me do was reconnect with The Zig Ziglar Corp. Zig Ziglar had spoken at my conference a few months earlier, and I met Tom and Julie Ziglar, but I hadn't followed up with them. I followed up and began to spend time with Tom. I began building a relationship with Ziglar. At that time, they had a worldwide video broadcast, and they asked me to speak to their audience about small-business growth.

As it turned out, Ziglar had fallen down the stairs and hit his head. He lost his short-term memory and eventually had to end his speaking career, which was the financial driver of their business at that time.

My company became the exclusive small-business coaching company for Ziglar, and the exposure to Ziglar's audience put me in front of business owners worldwide. Tom and I traveled the world together sharing the message of phenomenal business success.

Today, we coach in over a hundred different industries in twenty countries. Several of the coauthors of this book came to us through Ziglar.

As a result of building phenomenally successful businesses, I truly live a dream life. To have the influence and impact in other people's lives, helping them have breakthroughs in their business and life, is truly the most gratifying feeling you could ever imagine.

Today, Phenomenal Business Coaching is franchising our coaching and training processes. We currently have nine franchisees that are sharing phenomenal business strategies with others around the country. All the while, I enjoy time with my grandkids on my favorite beach. It is truly a dream life that every business owner can live, if they choose to do so.

About Howard

Howard Partridge is an international business coach with coaching members in over one hundred industries in twenty countries. He is a best-selling author of thirteen books, a TEDx speaker, the exclusive business coach for the Zig Ziglar Corp., the first Ziglar Legacy Trainer in the world, the first founding member of The John Maxwell Team, Donald Miller's first Business Made Simple Coach, and a Master DISC Certified Human Behavior Expert.

Howard grew up on welfare in Mobile, Alabama, and left home at eighteen. He arrived in Houston, Texas, on a Greyhound bus with only twenty-five cents in his pocket. He started his first business out of the trunk of his car in 1984 and built it into a multimillion-dollar enterprise. He has owned nine small businesses altogether and owns four companies at the time of this printing.

He is the president of Phenomenal Business Coaching, which helps small-business owners stop being slaves to their businesses by transforming them into predictable, profitable, turnkey operations.

Since 1998, Howard has helped small-business owners around the world dramatically improve their businesses.

He has led hundreds of seminars, webinars, and workshops, and holds his own live multiday events, which have featured some of America's top business trainers, including John Maxwell, Michael Gerber, Bob Burg, Dr. Joseph A. Michelli, Darren Hardy, Dr. Robert Rohm, and American legend Zig Ziglar.

Howard is married to Denise; has one son, Christian, and a daughter-in-love named Susana; and is a proud grandfather to Gianna and Elijah Partridge.

Get free videos, webinars, and resources for growing a phenomenal business and living a phenomenal L.I.F.E. at www.HowardPartridge.com.

CHAPTER 2

BUILT BY FAITH, DRIVEN BY PURPOSE

By Edwin Blosser

was thirteen the first time Jesus saved my life. And a few months later, He did it again.

The first time wasn't dramatic, at least not on the outside. There was no lightning strike, just a quiet conviction in my heart. A visiting minister had come and preached with a fire I'd never felt before. He said death would come for all of us, eternity only had two destinations, and that every soul makes a choice. I knew, at that moment, I hadn't yet made mine.

Even though I grew up in an Amish Mennonite church community I had not yet personally asked Jesus to be my Savior. I left that sermon with a strange, restless feeling. The next day out in the field with my father I asked him, "What does it mean, "God be merciful to me a sinner" and "What do I have to do to accept Jesus?"

That day, I gave my life to Christ and finally understood what it meant to be born again. Jesus became more than a name in a sermon. I was flooded with a peace I didn't want to lose. He became my Savior and guide. I attended instruction class that summer and was baptized in August. I felt like I was on top of the mountain! But November would bring a monumental moment!

Just a few months later, my neighbor Clarence and I were helping with the harvest. We first had to unload the wagon full of corn parked by the auger and sheared a pin in the unloading auger. We decided to take the tractor back home to get the shear pin which was ¾ mile down the road. I was driving the tractor. Clarence was riding on the back. As I drove onto the road, I glanced behind me and saw a pickup truck coming from a distance. I noticed it was gaining. *Fast.* I turned toward the side of the road to get out of the way, and increased the throttle to max., But it was too late. I heard Clarence scream, and the world went black.

When I came to, I was in a ditch, in front of the pickup. The tractor was split in two and the pickup had crashed with such force it ended up in front of the tractor. Clarence was draped over the hood, his leg nearly severed and sliding off down onto the road with a thump that I will never forget. I screamed his name and crawled to him, trying to make sense of the scene. Later, they told me I'd been thrown eighty-five feet through the air. The impact should've killed me. I should've been crushed beneath the weight of twisted steel, but I remember only a strange calm, like being carried by something soft and unseen and I knew exactly what it was.

Angels. God had saved my soul in May, and in November, He saved my life.

The driver of the pickup was dead, and Clarence died nine hours later. I remember thinking I might die, but I wasn't afraid because I knew where I was going. I'd made my choice. After the accident, I understood that I'd been spared for a reason.

At thirteen, I didn't know what that reason was, I just knew I'd felt the hand of God not once, but twice in the same year. It would take time for me to understood that God doesn't just save us *from* things, He saves us *for* things.

Follow the Breadcrumbs God Lays Before You

By 1980 my family had expanded our farming operation, but interest rates soared, and we were hit hard. My brothers and I worked day and night trying desperately to save the farm. The stress was constant. I prayed, "Lord, if there's a way I can help family farms thrive and not just survive—help me to be in it and truly help them."

In our community, formal education ended after eighth grade, but that didn't hinder me. I studied everything I could about soil biology, renewable and sustainable farming, and later learned about composting and why it can be so beneficial. I enrolled in programs and trained for more than seven years to become a certified soil practitioner. I learned to read soil, root systems, crop behavior, and water flow in both soils and plants. I started wondering, "How could we grow better food so both the farmers and consumers can live better lives?

In 1992, a colleague and I read an article about an Austrian doctor who had begun experimenting with enzymes and composting. His discoveries were astonishing. We organized a group of seven of us to go to Europe to meet him. Then, one by one everyone backed out. I knew in my spirit that God had called me to go, so I did. *Alone.* I'd never traveled internationally before and it was overwhelming, but God guided me and what I saw changed everything.

In Austria I met the doctor face-to-face. He had once been a conventional physician, but realized that he wasn't curing disease, he was simply managing symptoms. He began studying nutrition and discovered that the effective nutrition of food was directly tied to the vitality of the soil it was grown in, and most modern soil was severely depleted. More specifically, he discovered the power of enzymes—invisible agents that regulate digestion, immunity, cellular repair, and more. When soil lacked enzyme-rich activity, the food grown from it lacked the nutrition and resulting enzyme activity that human bodies need to thrive.

He left medicine, became a farmer and after years of struggle, transformed his land using humus-rich compost to produce food that healed the body. He took me to several farms applying his methods. I dug my hand into his wheat field and felt soft, living soil all the way to my elbow. I examined cows being fed Humus-enriched food and was astonished at how healthy they were. Enzymes coming from the Humus Proteins he made in the compost weren't just plant nutrition; they were the bridge between earth and human vitality. In other words, highly effective nutritious food becomes therapeutic in aiding people's bodies to heal themselves.

When I came home from Europe, I'd seen the future, and knew I had a role to play. That vision became Midwest Bio Systems.

We began designing and manufacturing the *Aeromaster Composting Equipment*—machines that could help farmers create high-quality, biologically active compost more efficiently and affordably; compost that could restore land, increase yields, improve livestock health, and even impact the nutritional value of food.

Today, our systems are used in 31 countries. We've trained many growers to revitalize their operations, reduce costs, and regenerate their soil. But what matters most to me isn't market reach—it's *mission* reach.

I want farmers to succeed because I know what it's like to almost lose everything. Looking back, I see the breadcrumbs God left for me: The sermon. The accident. The renewable farming training. The Austrian doctor.

God didn't hand me a blueprint. He handed me the next step, and I took it. I sometimes took it apprehensively, but what I thought was just survival turned out to be preparation. What looked like a delay was divine strategy.

If you're lost, follow the breadcrumbs and trust that God doesn't waste anything. He rewrites stories, repurposes scars, and turns brokenness into blessings.

THE POWER OF TRUSTING THE SOLUTION

In the summer of 1995 I received a fax that took my breath away. Our European marketing organization decided to stop selling our equipment. We had ten complete machines and ten more half-built. If I didn't find a way to sell the machines, we were finished. That was the moment I learned that in business and in life you must always know the lay of the land. Not just the opportunities, but the risks. Not just what you stand to gain, but what your recourse is if things go wrong. I had been so focused on what we *could* do with that partner company that I hadn't calculated what we *would* do if the deal fell apart. When the worst happened, I had no safety net except one: *faith.* I believed that God had not been caught off guard. The same God who had saved me at thirteen would not leave me now.

I've learned that it's a mistake to spend your energy fighting the situation you're in. You must accept what's outside your control and focus on what's within it. What I could control was my response, my creativity, and my decision to believe there was a way forward.

One of the urgent tasks we needed to handle was the renaming of our brand. We felt it was risky to keep the old brand name for the compost turners. A friend asked, "What's the one thing that sets your machines apart?" I answered, "The air exchange system." He nodded. "Call it the Aeromaster!" That moment birthed a new chapter, a new name, a new beginning. We sold the machines and recovered. That situation taught me not to panic when doors slam shut. Closed doors could be divine protection, and every crisis carries the seed of a solution.

Now, before every major decision, I ask myself: What's the risk? What's my backup plan? But most of all, what do you want me to do Lord? We are called to walk by faith, yes, but not with our eyes closed. There is *always* a solution. It may not be the one you expected or look like success right away. But if you keep your eyes open, your heart aligned, and your pride in check, you'll find it.

What to Do When Faced with a Challenge

In 2008 I faced another crisis. What I didn't realize then was that the Latin root of the word "crisis" means "a turning point." Crisis was God's invitation to trust Him more deeply. This crisis came in the form of a 75 percent drop in sales practically overnight. Our bank gave us an ultimatum: we had fifty-six days to make a $352,000 payment. I remember our CFO telling me, "There's no earthly way you can do this." He was right—there was no *earthly* way. But I'd seen enough by then to know that heaven works best when earth runs out. I left the office and became a full-time salesperson.

I hit the road with a fire in my bones. I logged over one hundred thousand miles that year, not just chasing down deals but transferring my enthusiasm in our product. I discovered that passion is contagious, and presence builds trust.

During that time, I struggled but didn't give up, and God wouldn't either. On the fifty-second day, with just four days left, we had enough sales to make the payment. It was a miracle. One day, at my lowest mentally and emotionally, my friend Eric showed up. I told him that I was discouraged, and he asked me a question I'll never forget: "Have you thanked God for this struggle?" I responded honestly that I didn't see much to be grateful for! That night, I prayed: "God, I don't feel thankful—but I want to be. I thank You for this trial." I repeated that prayer hundreds of times since then. Within days, the cloud started to lift.

During the two years that followed, I experienced more miracles than at any other point in my life. God wasn't just rescuing me from disaster—He was drawing me into *relationship* and teaching me to thank Him even for the trials. Every hardship is an invitation to go deeper—not just in strategy, but in *Spirit*. We often want the breakthrough without the burden, but I've learned that God hides some of His greatest gifts inside the hardest moments.

THE RED THREAD: FAITH AND GRATITUDE

If I had to name the thread that runs through every season of my life it would be this: Gratitude and faith. Not just when things go right, but especially when they don't. Of all the experiences that shaped who I am today, perhaps none changed me more than the life and passing of our son, Denver John Blosser.

Denver was born in 1998 with special needs, following birth complications. He was a *gift*. A radiant, humbling, joy-filled gift.

Denver's mental capacity was limited, but his spirit was strong.

His childlike faith could brighten the hardest day. He didn't understand the details of my work, he just wanted to be with me. Whether I was in a meeting, or just trying to think through a problem, he was happy to just be in my presence. On May 1, 2020, Denver came to the office one more time. That day, when I told him lunch was ready, he jumped up, ran to the van, and began singing at the top of his lungs: "Safely now, I'm home with Jesus…" I would normally ask him to quiet down, but this time, I opened the window and let his song fill the air. Then, he laid his hand on my arm, and said, "If I go to be with Jesus, I don't have to come back, right?" "No," I said gently, never imagining those words would be answered only hours later. Just past 1:30 am that night, Denver passed peacefully in his sleep.

Many factors contributed to my awareness of my own proneness to failure and frailty, I am not the same man I was before he came, nor the same man I was before I nearly lost everything—more than once. Most of all, the most dramatic change came after I understood what it means to be grateful for struggle and faithful to God's plan.

With God's Blessings our extraordinary business allows me to carry out God's purpose for my life, but what's most important to me aren't the sales quotas, the recognition or the legacy. What matters is that I remember who Jesus wants me to be: a leader who never gives up, never loses faith and always practices gratitude. Romans 8:28 isn't just a verse I quote, it's the blueprint of my life: "All things work together for good to those who love God."

At this point in my life, every morning when I wake up, I thank God for loving me, and I am starting the habit of saying "Great things are always happening for me every day." It's not wishful thinking. It's faith in motion. It's the kind of belief that drove me to build machines from nothing; to keep going after loss, struggle and heartache; and to be the kind of father, man, and servant my family and community need me to be.

That's what all of this has taught me: That God's greatest work is often done in the soil of our struggle, and if we trust Him, even our pain can become a pathway to purpose, a source of strength, and the doorway to solutions.

About Edwin

Edwin Blosser is a farmer, inventor, and man of deep faith who believes all things are possible *through grace*. His life was transformed at thirteen when Jesus saved both his soul and his life just three months apart, a defining year that became the cornerstone of everything he would later build.

Raised in an Amish-Mennonite home and trained through years of hands-on learning, Edwin became a pioneer in biological soil health. He founded Midwest Bio-Systems, and he developed and manufactures the Aeromaster Composting Equipment, now used in over thirty countries to help farmers and commercial composters reduce input costs, regenerate soil, and improve the health of their land both naturally and efficiently.

Edwin's *why* is clear: *Success happens when we make sense of the complex*. He lives that out by seeking depth, details, and understanding in every challenge, which allows him to design practical solutions that bring lasting impact to the farming community. His work is driven by the belief that God doesn't just save us *from* things—He saves us *for* things.

But it's not the equipment that defines Edwin's legacy; it's his humility, his faith, and his gratitude. By remaining honest about his failures and aware of human frailty, Edwin has discovered that true greatness is found not in control but in surrender. Through trials, miracles, and the grace of God, he has built a life and business anchored in purpose.

Learn more at MidwestBioSystems.com.

CHAPTER 3

FROM BREAKDOWN TO BREAKTHROUGH

Building a Life and Business That Matter

By Nathan Shafer

"**Y**ou've got to get home right now."

Something in my mother-in-law's tone stopped me in my tracks.

I was standing on a job site, hands covered in dust, training a new guy on the crew, when the call had come. "Bri's in the shower," she said, "And Tate won't wake up."

My heart seemed to stop. My two-year-old son was unresponsive? I jumped in the truck and raced home. As I pulled into the driveway, an ambulance was pulling out. I barely recognized my own son—his tiny face swollen beyond recognition and his body totally limp.

At the hospital, the doctors worked fast. His blood sugar had plummeted to nearly nothing. We spent days in an agonizing blur of fear and helplessness. We got him home, but the doctors were unable to find a cause and it was far from over. Three more episodes followed. Imagine having no idea what is causing your child to not wake up and therefore no idea what to avoid. Every time I held him, I wondered if I'd wake up the next day with my boy still breathing.

And then, as suddenly as it had started, it stopped. That was 10 years ago, and he has been fine ever since.

But I wasn't the same man after that. Something happens when you come that close to losing what matters most. It rewires you. It forces you to see what you've been blind to all along.

For me, it was this: I had spent my whole life working in our family's HVAC business. Ten years full-time. I had consistently worked eighty hours a week, sacrificing time, energy, and my family for a business that, while successful, wasn't giving me the life I had envisioned. I had always dreamed of something bigger—a thriving company, a strong team, a life where I wasn't drowning in work just to keep the wheels turning. But I was stuck.

Watching that ambulance pull out of my driveway with my son in the back, I was hit with brutal clarity: If I kept doing things the way we always had, I would never have the life I wanted. My business would always own me instead of me owning it. My family would always get my leftovers instead of my best. That was the breaking point, and I knew one thing. It had to start with me. I had to lead this change. And I had to find someone to show me the way.

SUCCESS IS NOT A ONE-MAN SHOW

A few years ago, after joining the Phenomenal Business Coaching community, I heard my coach, Howard Partridge, share a powerful distinction he learned from the legendary Zig Ziglar—the difference between success and significance. Zig taught that success is having more of the good things in life—more money, more freedom, more of what you enjoy. But significance is about helping *others* be, do, and have more of the good things in life. That concept struck me hard. Like many entrepreneurs, I had achieved what most would call "success." On the outside, we had the things people associate with winning in life—a growing business, material possessions, the ability to travel, horses, competing in rodeos and experiences many dream of. And yet, for me, it wasn't enough.

The game changed for me when I shifted my focus inward and became committed to growing *myself* as a leader. That's when fulfillment started to show up. I discovered that my greatest joy didn't come from what I could accumulate but from who I was becoming and how it was helping others succeed. Spending time with family and helping someone reach their personal and professional goals was, to me, significance.

Zig summed it up perfectly when he said, "You can have everything in life you want if you will just help enough other people get what they want." That's the business I'm in now—helping people win. I realized that to play a bigger and more fulfilling game, I needed help.

If I was going to become the leader my family, my team, and my community needed, I had to make a decision. Becoming self-aware enough to know when you need help isn't weakness—it's wisdom. The most successful people in the world don't do it alone. They seek out mentors, coaches, and communities that stretch them, challenge them, and support their growth. So, I did something that scared me. I hired a business coach.

I didn't know how we were going to afford it at the time. But I took the leap. I placed a bet on myself, my family, and my future. And thank God I did. Because not long after, the world turned upside down.

STAYING SOLUTION FOCUSED

In the second half of 2019, hiring a business coach felt counterintuitive. It was a huge investment, but something in me knew I needed help. I had reached the point where working harder wasn't going to cut it anymore. I wrote the check, hoping I had made a solid investment.

Then came 2020.

I remember it like it was yesterday. It was early March, and COVID was shutting down the world. My parents and I sat at the boardroom table shellshocked by the sudden turn of events and the grim reality that came with it. What would we do now? Who were we going to lay off on Monday? These weren't just employees—these were people we cared about with families who relied on us. I left the meeting heavy-hearted and headed to a job site feeling frustrated and afraid. Once I got there, I noticed that the guys had installed something backwards and I snapped. I stormed back to the truck and did the best thing I could have done—I called my coach.

I told him everything: how scared I was, how we didn't know what to do, how layoffs seemed inevitable. I unloaded it all. He listened quietly and then asked me the question that changed everything: "What can you control right now?" That simple question transformed my mindset. Up until that moment, my mind was consumed with fear, the "what ifs," the worst-case scenarios playing out on the news. He told me to stop watching the news and to stop feeding my mind with negativity. What *was* within my control? How I showed up. How I led my team. How I chose to think. Within that one phone call, my mindset shifted. I walked back onto that job site a completely different person. The guys were stunned. One of them even asked, "What are you smoking? You were furious an hour ago, now you're laughing."

From that moment forward, I chose to be solution-focused—to control what I could control. And the result? We never laid a single person off. Instead, we grew. We added two more team members that year and grew the business by 87 percent in revenue and 800 percent in net profit—right in the middle of a global pandemic. It wasn't smooth sailing. There were constant challenges—supply chain issues, delayed parts, trucks we couldn't get and employees calling off sick, but every time a problem hit, we asked the same question: "What can we control and what's the solution?"

We found new vendors, turned a building into a warehouse, bought equipment when we had the cash and sold what we could to stay three steps ahead. We didn't sit back—we got proactive. That mindset—Positive Attitude—became one of our core values. For us, it means a *"We Will Overcome"* attitude. And we did overcome. Year after year, we continued to grow. We made the INC5000 list twice. We surpassed our budgets and even hit our stretch goal in 2022, celebrating with a team-paid, all-inclusive trip to the Bahamas—a dream come true.

The bottom line is that you are either an addition sign, a

subtraction sign, or a division sign in every room you walk into. And what determines that is your mindset. Growth comes when you discipline yourself to see the opportunity in every obstacle and choose to lead from that place, no matter what. Because in business, and in life, it's not the challenges that define you—it's how you choose to respond.

The Power of Relationships

I've always heard Zig Ziglar say, "Your network is your net worth." Like many people, I understood it conceptually—but I didn't truly see the power of that principle until I began intentionally surrounding myself with top leaders in my industry. When I did, door after door began opening—personally and professionally.

The truth is, you never know who someone knows or where a single connection can take you. Relationships are the true currency of business and life. For example, long before I met my business coach, Howard Partridge, I knew Ellen Rohr. If you're in the plumbing and trades industry, you know Ellen—she's well-respected and widely known. Over the years, Ellen often spoke about Howard. Out of curiosity, I looked him up.

Years later, after my first coach sold his business, I found myself at a crossroads. I knew the value of mentorship and knew I couldn't—and shouldn't—do this journey alone. That's when Howard popped into my head. I made the call. And looking back, that one decision, built entirely on a relationship, has been life changing. If it weren't for Ellen, I would have never met Howard. And through Howard, countless doors have opened.

Since meeting him, I've had the privilege of meeting and spending time one-on-one with industry icons like Brian Tracy, Michael Gerber, and many other top leaders. But it wasn't just business doors that opened. My relationships with Howard and my first coach created a ripple effect. It forced me to take a hard look at the relationships closest to me—my family, my team, the people I do life with every day.

That's where DISC came in—and it became one of the most

transformative tools I've ever used. If you're unfamiliar with DISC, it's a behavioral assessment that breaks down personality styles into four main types—Dominant, Inspiring, Supportive, and Cautious. It's not about right or wrong—it's about understanding yourself and others at a deeper level. We all have strengths and blind spots. DISC taught me how I'm wired and why I react the way I do under pressure. Like a lot of business owners, I'm a high "D" personality. Dominant. Driven. Competitive. The kind of person who pushes hard, expects results, and doesn't have a lot of patience for excuses. But here's the problem: if you don't understand that about yourself, it can show up as being pushy, aggressive, or impatient. You risk steamrolling the very people you're supposed to be leading. The truth is, people want to win, but they don't all define winning the same way you do. That was a huge wake-up call for me.

Through two levels of DISC certification with Dr. Robert Rohm, I learned how to harness that drive and passion and communicate it effectively. I learned the power of asking questions, and listening not to respond but to truly understand. I stopped telling people what to do and started asking how we could win together. I learned that while money motivates me, it doesn't motivate everyone the same way. So, we gamified the business. We created different rewards tied to goals, not just financial but experiences and celebrations that meant something to *them*.

Today, I lead with transparency. My team knows when we're winning and exactly *how* much we're winning. And they know when we're losing, too. Why? Because I want them to have ownership in the outcome—without bearing the risks I carry as the owner. I tell them all the time, "This business is your vehicle, too. Let it take you where you want to go in life."

Relationships—whether personal or professional—thrive when you understand yourself first. When you know what drives you, what challenges you, and how you show up under pressure, you can start leading people the way *they* need to be led—not just the way you like to lead. That's what turns a group of individuals into a winning team and a business into a legacy.

Stay Plugged In

Looking back, one of the biggest mistakes I made early on was isolating myself when things got hard. I didn't recognize the warning signs soon enough. We were experiencing rapid growth, and I kept thinking, "This will pass. I just need to work harder." The truth is, working harder isn't always the answer. Sometimes it's what keeps you stuck. For me, it took my son getting sick to snap me out of it.

Here's what I know now: you cannot win in business or life if you isolate yourself.

Especially when things get tough, your instinct is to hunker down, grind harder, and try to outwork the problem. But that only makes it worse. You lose perspective and support.

The real key is staying plugged in—to your mentors, your colleagues, your friends, your faith, and your goals. Surround yourself with positive, like-minded people who remind you what you're capable of and push you to stay solution-focused when the pressure is on. That's how you build a business that lasts.

I learned this firsthand. After several years of growth, my parents could retire and that allowed me to purchase the business. But what followed was one of the hardest years of my life.

There were tough financial lessons, administrative headaches, shifts in the economy, changes in the industry, and plenty of sleepless nights. But I stayed plugged in, leaned into the lessons, and kept my mindset right. We came back the following year leaner, stronger, clearer and grew our revenue by 50 percent and our profits by almost 130 percent with nearly the same overhead and a few less people. That's the power of staying connected. That's what happens when you keep sharpening your tools, your mindset, and your relationships. For me, leadership is about service. I genuinely care about my team, our clients, and the community we're blessed to serve. Whether it's showing up for strategic planning, or giving back through veterans' initiatives and community events, I lead with service.

And above all, I keep God first—in my life, in my relationships, and in our business. Every single day starts with prayer as a team because I believe that foundation is what keeps us grounded, focused, and aligned. If there's one thing I want you to take away from this chapter, it's this: When you hit a wall, don't panic—pivot. Lean *in*, not *out*. That's how you turn things around. That's how you turn adversity into advantage. And that's how you build not just a phenomenal business—but a phenomenal life.

About Nathan

Nathan Shafer grew up working in his family's HVAC business, where he dedicated himself as an operator. Despite the hard work, the business plateaued at $1.4 million in annual revenue with ten team members. Like many small-business owners, Nathan found himself overwhelmed, working twelve-to-sixteen-hour days, seven days a week, and struggling to find good help.

Determined to break free from this cycle, Nathan decided to step away from daily operations and focus on growing the business. He sought guidance from coaches and mentors, which led to remarkable transformation. In just three years Nathan's HVAC company skyrocketed to $6.5 million in revenue, expanded to thirty team members, and was listed as one of America's fastest-growing privately owned companies, earning a spot on the Inc. 5000 list for two consecutive years. The company has also been a Great Place to Work Certified for multiple years in a row, along with other humbling industry awards.

With a robust system in place, Nathan now enjoys more family time, fewer daily challenges, and a talented team ready for growth.

Inspired by his journey and the mentorship of Howard Partridge, Nathan joined Phenomenal Business Coaching in 2022 and later acquired the franchise in 2023. He is passionate about sharing his experiences and helping other small-business owners escape the grind through effective leadership, administration, marketing, sales, and operations coaching.

Visit this link to access free training: Winwithnathan.com.

Follow him on Facebook: www.facebook.com/share/16UMp3qaMf/?m ibextid=wwXIfr.

CHAPTER 4

PHENOMENAL STRUGGLE BREEDS PHENOMENAL SUCCESS

By Nick Nanton

I could tell by the tone of my CFO's voice that he wasn't calling with good news.

Christmas was just two weeks away, but there was no merriment or holiday spirit in his greeting, just a flat, direct tone that immediately made my heart start racing.

"Well, Nick," he said, allowing me a moment to brace for the worst, "you better pull a rabbit out of the hat, or we're not making payroll." Awesome. Merry Christmas to me.

The weird part? Six months earlier we were flying high! We were having our best creative year yet and had more money in the bank than we had ever had before. It felt as if we were bulletproof. Turns out we were just a few perfectly misaligned events away from a full-blown disaster.

That was years ago, and thankfully we survived, but looking back, that period of time held valuable lessons. You see, it wasn't bad leadership or laziness. It wasn't even some major screwup. It was just life doing what life does best: throwing a wrench into the gears at the worst possible time. Still, knowing it wasn't *technically* my fault didn't stop the voices in my head that taunted, "You're better than this. You should have seen it coming. You're a failure."

I smiled through Christmas parties while mentally

43

hyperventilating. How could this be? The week before that phone call was like a highlight reel of my wildest dreams. I had flown to LA, cut a deal to work on a huge record, hit an awards show where one of our documentaries was nominated for a massive industry award, and then jetted off to meet my family in New York City to take in the lights, and all the while things had been falling apart.

Here's the thing they don't tell you about success: The highlights are real but so are the stomach-turning, sometimes almost paralyzing, moments. Jack Canfield has a principle that basically says: "Take 100 percent responsibility for everything in your life. Even when you're not."

At some point you stop whining, stop wishing, and just ask, "What can I do right now?" Not, "Who's to blame?" Not, "Why me?" Just, "What's next?"

So I did what I had to do. I made the awkward calls. I asked for prepayments from partners with projects already in the works. I bared my teeth and my soul and basically threw every tool, favor, and Hail Mary I had at the problem. It wasn't fun. It sure as heck wasn't comfortable. But it worked. We made it. And if that experience taught me anything, it's this: Phenomenal success is built on the back of phenomenal struggle. There's no shortcut. No cheat code. No way around it.

You don't get the trophies without the tears. And when everything falls apart, and you feel like you've been thrown back to the starting line—that's not failure. That's preschool. That's the school of struggle, the original classroom where greatness is born. When you were first learning how to walk, you didn't quit the first time you fell on your face. You didn't think, "Well, guess I'm just not cut out for walking." You fell. You got up. You fell again. You struggled your way into strength. We just forget that as adults. Especially as business owners and leaders. We start expecting smooth roads and fair winds, and we get crushed the minute it doesn't go according to plan.

Here's the truth no one puts on a motivational poster: You have to *accept* the polarity. Success and struggle are a package deal.

You don't get one without the other. And there are some struggles that are just inherently built into the leadership path. The sooner you accept those struggles as a reality—whether you like them or not—the faster you'll get up the next time you get knocked flat. And you will get knocked flat. Again and again. That's not failure. That's the tuition you pay for phenomenal success.

REALITY 1: COMPARISON KILLS MOMENTUM

There's something we don't talk about enough in entrepreneurship: Comparison is not just the thief of joy—it's the thief of growth. Look, we're all carrying our own battle scars. I was an immigrant kid born into some financial struggles. That was my starting line. It was hard. But if you stack my story next to someone who survived abuse or extreme trauma, I can't help but argue that my hardship is lighter. Still—and this is the key—*the worst thing in your life is still the worst thing in your life.*

Pain isn't a competition. And while we should never minimize anyone else's hardship, there's no scoreboard or prize for who suffered most. The truth is we all have monsters. They just wear different masks. You can't compare your monster to someone else's. You can't shrink your scars because you think someone else had it worse—or bigger, or louder, or flashier. Your story is yours. Your path is yours. And it becomes your point of differentiation. It's what makes you, *you.* The minute you start measuring your journey against somebody else's—Richard Branson's, Gary Vee's, your neighbor's—you start losing two critical things: the lesson meant for *you,* and the strength you build by *living* it.

Here's the reality most people miss: The bigger the empire, the bigger the problems. Everyone is one bad decision, one economic shift, or one bad diagnosis away from a financial crisis. You think the rich and famous don't deal with family chaos? Court battles? Health scares? You think there's a level you get to where the monsters disappear? They don't. They just start wearing nicer shoes.

You were given your experiences, your intelligence, your pain tolerance for a reason. You're building the life *you* can handle. I once heard a quote that resonated with me that went something like this: "You earn in direct proportion to the amount of pain you're willing to withstand." Unless you inherit it, no one becomes a millionaire without walking through fires most people never see. The faster you stop comparing, the faster you level up. The tests you are given were built specifically for you. Live your own story, validate your own experiences. They are what makes you a category of one.

REALITY 2: STOP TAKING THE CYCLES PERSONALLY

If you grew up like I did—immigrant kid, financial trauma baked into your DNA—your brain gets wired a certain way. Scarcity becomes the default setting. You don't just think there might not be enough. You *know* there's not enough. That wiring doesn't just disappear because you "make it." It shows up later—sometimes louder than ever—when the stakes are higher and more people are depending on you.

At one point, I realized I had trained myself to *ignore* problems. Not because I didn't care. But because, deep down, I didn't believe I had the resources—mentally, financially, emotionally—to handle them if they blew up. So I chose not to participate. Stick my head in the sand. Hope for the best and pray that nothing caught fire. Spoiler alert: this is an extremely limited strategy. Eventually, I had to wake up to something brutal but freeing: Life and business are cyclical. Always have been. Always will be.

The stock market rises, falls, then rises again. The sun shines, the storm moves in, then the sun shines again. Everything in life is cyclical. Business. Emotions. Momentum. Money. All of it moves in seasons, not in straight lines. You can fight it if you want. You can waste your energy shouting at the rain. Or you can expect the storm and ride it out. Feast and famine aren't anomalies—they're baked into the structure. You can have the best product, the best team, the best year of your life, and still face a downturn that has nothing to do with you. Tariffs shift. AI disrupts your entire category overnight. You sell winter jackets, and the next winter is the hottest on record. You can hustle your face off and you still cannot lower the temperature enough to sell more jackets.

If you expect to always crush it, you'll start thinking you're failing when you're actually just in a natural dip. It's not *you*. It's the season you're in. And if you're not careful, you'll internalize every valley like it's some giant neon flashing FAILURE sign. The best move? Build a war chest. You need enough margin—cash, energy, time, strategy—so when the storm comes, you can *pay attention* and *pivot* instead of running on fumes and cortisol. You need enough capacity to think, not just survive. This is of course easier advice to give than to receive. Because success isn't about avoiding cycles, it's about respecting them. When you stop taking the cycles personally, you stop doubting yourself every time the tide goes out. And you stop confusing weather patterns with self-worth.

REALITY 3: YOU'RE GOING TO HIT THE GROUND—LEARN TO LIKE IT!

When you can stop seeing every setback as a cosmic injustice and start seeing it as an essential feature of the game everything changes. Steven Kotler talks about this idea in *The Rise of Superman*. He tells a story about a professional skateboarder who said the only reason he got as good as he did was because he fell in love with the ground! He didn't just tolerate falling. He *celebrated* it. Every wipeout wasn't a failure, it was a trophy; proof he was pushing the edge of what was possible. Ray Dalio, one of the most successful investors of all time, calls this the "good struggle." Not good outcomes. Not good luck. Good *struggle*.

It's not about winning every time. It's about becoming the kind of person who's not afraid of the hard things. The kind of person who understands that pain is a teacher and that setbacks are just data. The idea is to come to a place where you can feel that falling flat on your face isn't something to be ashamed of—it's something to be *grateful* for. Because if you're falling, it means you're moving. You're taking shots most people are too scared to even try. You're playing for something bigger than comfort. The ground is not your enemy. It's your launchpad.

REALITY 4: YOU WILL BE STRANDED ON AN ISLAND

Here's something nobody puts in the entrepreneurship brochure: It's lonely at the top. It's lonely in the middle, too. Heck, it's lonely at every level if you're doing it right.

Bill Glazer—who built a legendary empire with Dan Kennedy—said it straight: "The entrepreneur is the loneliest person in the world." And he wasn't being dramatic. He was telling the truth. When you're running a business, you're walking a tightrope every day. When you're in a downswing, you're scared, but you can't dump your fear on your employees, or you'll freak them out or start a mass exodus. You don't want to worry your family either. They can't fix it. They'll just lose sleep.

When you're in an upswing, you're excited, but you have to be careful how you celebrate because success can trigger all kinds of weird expectations. People may think you've got endless money and start lining up for raises, bonuses, handouts—when deep down, you know the truth: this could all vanish tomorrow.

The bigger the swings, the bigger the responsibility. And the harder it becomes to know who you can *actually* talk to. Most people won't get it. Unless they've signed payroll checks themselves. Unless they've laid awake at 3 a.m. wondering if they're one bad week away from losing it all. Unless they've ridden the insane rollercoaster that is building something out of thin air. That's why if you want to survive you have to build your circle.

You need a support network made of other leaders, mentors and people you can be *unfiltered* with. You need people you can high-five on your good days and lament with on your bad ones; people who don't flinch when you say, "I'm terrified," or, "I just closed the biggest deal of my life and now I'm scared I'll blow it." You need places where you can share both sides of the coin—without guilt, without shame, without spin. Because you're not actually alone, you're just playing a bigger game than most people are willing to.

THE PRICE AND PRIZE OF BEING PHENOMENAL

If there's one truth you can carve into stone, it's this: Phenomenal success comes from phenomenal struggle. There's no way around it. Only through. But let's be real—*struggle* feels like the wrong word. It sounds too heavy and honestly like something most of us would work hard to avoid. The truth is what we call struggle is really something else entirely: It's *forging.*

Struggle isn't here to break you. It's here to *forge* you into something stronger, sharper, more unstoppable than you were before. Forging is the furnace where greatness gets built.

And you've got to be able to hold that level of responsibility. When the numbers get bigger, the wins are sweeter, and the falls hit harder. A $500 mistake becomes a $500,000 mistake. A small panic becomes a full-blown crisis. That's the tradeoff. That's the cost of entry.

In my own life, I've stood in the fire. I've gone negative on a credit line and had to claw my way back. I've lived the gut-punch of seeing a high-flying year suddenly nosedive without warning. And if I hadn't learned the mindset and developed the grit to keep swinging, the heart to keep standing, or the guts to keep showing up, I wouldn't be here. Success doesn't go to the smartest person, or the luckiest or even the most talented. It goes to the person who can stay standing the longest. There's a quote I keep coming back to: "Genius is often just persistence in disguise." That's the game. Not who can win when everything's easy. Who can keep going when it's not.

If you want phenomenal success, you have to get good at handling phenomenal forging. You have to trust the process—the rising, the falling, the failing, the fighting—because it's carving you into the person who can hold the dream you say you want.

You get to the top of one mountain and inevitably you see a higher mountaintop that becomes your new goal. That's the human condition. You are probably sore at that moment, and you've no doubt been cursing the elevation and the climb the whole time. But once you reach that peak, you get a burst of energy and start forgetting about the pain of the climb. Your next choice is up to you: stay at that peak or go for the next one. And if you're like most entrepreneurs, I know what you're going to do.

Just remember as you embark on that next pursuit, you don't get to the top of the next mountain without eventually learning to love the climb.

About Nick

From the slums of Port-au-Prince, Haiti, with special forces raiding a sex trafficking ring and freeing children, to the Virgin Galactic Space Port in Mojave with Sir Richard Branson, twenty-two-time Emmy Award–winning Director-Producer Nick Nanton has become known for telling stories that connect. Why? Because he focuses on the most fascinating subject in the world: *people*. As an award-winning songwriter, storyteller, and best-selling author, Nick has shared his message with millions of people through his documentaries, speeches, blogs, lectures, songs, and best-selling books. Nick's book *StorySelling* hit The Wall Street Journal Best-Seller List and is available on Audible as an audiobook. Nick has directed more than sixty documentaries and a sold-out Broadway Show (garnering forty-three Emmy nominations in multiple regions and twenty-two wins), including:

- *DICKIE V* (ESPN/Disney+)
- *Rudy Ruettiger: The Walk On* (Amazon Prime)
- *The Rebound* (Netflix)
- *Operation Toussaint* (Amazon Prime)

Nick has shared the stage with, coauthored books with, and made films featuring:

- Larry King
- Kathie Lee Gifford
- Hoda Kotb
- Dick Vitale
- Kenny Chesney
- Magic Johnson
- Coach Mike Krzyzewski
- Jack Nicklaus
- Tony Robbins
- Lisa Nichols
- Peter Diamandis
- And many more

Nick specializes in bringing the element of human connection to every viewer, no matter the subject. He is currently directing and hosting the series *In Case You Didn't Know* (season 1 executive produced by Larry King), featuring legends in the worlds of business, entrepreneurship, personal development, technology, and sports.

Nick's first love has always been music. He has been writing songs for more than two decades, and his songs have been aired on radio across the

United States and in Canada. He is currently ranked in the top 10 percent of songwriters in the world. His songs have been recorded by Lee Brice, Darius Rucker, RaeLynn, Joe Bryson, and many more, and have amassed more than three million streams on Spotify, Apple Music, Pandora, and SoundCloud. He received three Gold records in 2018 for his work with the global touring band A Day to Remember.

Nick has written and/or produced songs that have appeared on the following shows or in promotional commercials for:

- the Fox prime-time series *Glee*, *New Girl*, *House*, and *Hell's Kitchen*
- the MLB All-Star Game
- ABC Family's hit series *Falcon Beach*
- the CBS prime-time series *Ghost Whisperer* starring Jennifer Love Hewitt

CHAPTER 5

THE PAIN AND PLEASURE OF SUBMITTING TO THE PROCESS OF GOD'S PERFECT PLAN

By Michael Acerra

I stepped off the plane in Ukraine in the middle of winter, dressed like I'd just wandered off a beach in Bali—which, truthfully, I had. I had no idea at that moment that it would be a future war zone, or that my future family and I would be in the middle of it.

I'd left behind paradise to chase something I couldn't explain, only feel: the certainty that my soulmate was standing on the other side of an airport terminal eager to celebrate her birthday together. When I finally saw her after a year of video chats and calls during the pandemic, we were both very happy. Ninety days later, we were married, and our beautiful daughter Aliia was on her way. When you know, you know.

We honeymooned in Bali for the summer then returned to Ukraine to prepare my newly adopted son, Eli, for the fall semester. We made the decision to get settled into our new life together in Ukraine, which was very different from living in Bali and Texas. Extensive renovations were started on our apartment, and I officially became an international businessman with the signing of my first contract. It was one thing to be a general contractor back home, but this was a whole new challenge for me in Europe especially when most people in my area did not speak English.

We were so excited to get everything ready for our baby, and this was one of the happiest times of my life. I was living my dream of being a family man; and it was fun spending time with my family getting familiar with Ukrainian culture. It was also a time when a lot of pressure was put on me to overcome obstacles that were presenting themselves back in Texas.

This led to the difficult decision to go back to the States at the end of October for a few weeks to tie up loose ends and get things in order praying that my daughter would not come before her late January due date. I had been living abroad for a year and there were things I needed to take care of in person like seeing my grandfather. My intuition told me that I needed to see him, and I found out later that it was correct once again.

We had made great progress on our remodeling and my wife stepped up to manage the workers while I was away. Being away from my family was very difficult for me and I was eager to get back to them as soon as possible. It was brought to my attention before I was about to travel back to my new home that Russia was about to invade Ukraine. This was also stated to me right before we married back in May, but there were zero signs of it while I was there, and I would never have known if people back home did not voice their concerns. This time it felt different and more credible. Every instinct in me screamed to go back and get my family. I remember saying goodbye to my friends and family, knowing full well that I may never see them again.

Love is one of the only things that will make you run headfirst into a war zone. If it was my time to go, then I would be leaving this earth with my family in Ukraine and would have no regrets.

Once I got back to them, the writing was on the wall, but our daughter was not here yet, and my wife felt that the Russians would leave the border as they did before. A few weeks later, Aliia was born, and 4 weeks after that our lives changed forever. The Russians invaded and destroyed all the airports which left us with only two viable options to escape, by car or train. They both had their risks, but we ultimately chose the train, which we learned later was the right choice. We had to get out before the army destroyed the railroads and we became prisoners of war or worse. Seeing the reality of war is something that I will never forget, and it puts a whole new perspective on the blessing of waking up each day. My grandfather passed away a week before the invasion, proving my intuition to see him was right once again.

Commercial flights weren't an option, and the roads were jammed with vehicles abandoned for miles. The gas stations had a limited supply of fuel, and they were overwhelmed with long lines of Ukrainians hoping to fuel up before they sold out. So we packed up a couple of backpacks and left everything behind in our newly renovated apartment. We still do not know if we will ever get to see it again or enjoy any of the new appliances that we didn't even get the chance to use. We readied our son and four-week-old daughter and crammed onto a train with hundreds of strangers, all of us pressed together like cattle. I'm a big guy, normally that counts for something, but that day, I was just one more body in a sea of panic trying to remain calm and protect my family. My wife had our daughter in her stroller in front of me while I tried to keep my son from being trampled from the mob of people rushing us from behind. I will never forget the terrifying moment my wife and daughter made it on board first with the help of an older gentleman who was saying goodbye to his daughter while my son and I were separated from them because of the crowd.

The miracle of getting on that train after my wife explained that we were left behind and pleaded with them not to leave us was only the beginning of our dangerous journey. There could be no phone use, no lights, and no noise. The slightest shine from a phone screen could alert the enemy to our whereabouts. It was silent other than the sounds of breathing, fear, and the occasional muffled sobs from women and children who realized that they may never see the men in their family again. The train ride to Lviv lasted almost twenty hours and was extremely uncomfortable, but my thoughts immediately went back to all the people who were left at the station who would gladly trade places with me in a second. This gave me the gratitude I needed to endure everything and stay focused on being grateful. There was little food, and the bathroom was not an option. Men between eighteen and sixty are not allowed to leave Ukraine and were forced to enlist. There were severe consequences for anyone attempting to flee and the ones who stayed but did not enlist would be snatched off the street then forced to fight. You could be going to the market for food and then that same day end up on the front lines fighting in the war. As an expat, I was an exception and did my best to help the many women and children who had been forced to flee without their husbands and sons. No matter how many news segments you saw about this war, nothing captured the reality of the horror taking place there and the torture being inflicted on innocent families and children.

When we finally crossed into Poland by bus from Lviv, the chaos lifted. Roads lined with people handing out food like we had seen in Ukraine on our journey to the border. Volunteers welcomed us like family. We cried, not from fear anymore—but from sheer relief and gratitude. I am forever grateful to Poland and Romania for helping Ukraine.

FOLLOWING THE BREADCRUMBS

Looking back now, I see that there were breadcrumbs scattered across my life, each one placed by a hand bigger than mine. At the time, it didn't feel like divine orchestration. It felt like hardship and pain. I was able to not only reflect on the most recent hardship we had overcome together as man and wife but also make sense of ones I had made it through before even meeting my wife. The similarities in our childhood hardships and sacrifices even though we were thousands of miles apart in different countries were one of the many things that showed us we were soulmates.

In 2009 I had just graduated into a recession. My car was in an accident and was considered a total loss. I was told I'd be paid the $31,000 insurance policy limit. Then they changed their mind and issued a denial letter. No car. No money. No safety net. This was the first rock bottom moment of my life, and I felt like a mas-sive failure taking a minimum wage job at a gym after getting my degree. I had to get rides to and from work which made matters worse. It was a punch to the gut, and I didn't know then what I know now: they owed me that money. Had I known who and what to ask, I could have spared myself many months of hardship. The irony? That moment would become the exact fuel for what I do now. Today, I am a public insurance adjuster helping people get what they're rightly owed from their insurance company. I'm licensed for auto, but I mostly handle property claims. Funny how God lets you become a victim long enough to teach you how to help someone else become a victor through your advocacy and testimonial.

I never set out to be a claims adjuster. I was recruited by a staffing agency and did not even know what an insurance adjuster was at the time, or that I would be climbing roofs most of the time. I stumbled into the industry by what I considered at the time to be an accident. I ended up staying, traveling the country and grinded through hundred-hour weeks. This was while I pursued my MBA and secured the foundation for my first business. I had to start the company in secret because they would have made me choose between being an employee or being self-employed, which would have been more difficult without the safety net. I also needed time to learn and develop my skills in the industry.

By January of 2012 I officially launched my roofing company as a side hustle and got my MBA in December at twenty-five. I hustled knowing that one day I would build myself up enough to leave my role as a claims adjuster. This would allow me to become a serial entrepreneur and eventually leave something behind; a legacy instead of a liability my future family could be proud of. In 2014 I gave up the corporate car, the benefits, and the illusion of stability. The company I was working for went through the acquisition of their largest competitor and grossly mismanaged it, which resulted in a shortage of resources and massively warped expectations. By then, I was already making more on weekends doing roofing work and installing Christmas lights, so I was confident taking a stand for myself whenever their demands of me were unreasonable. I finally was making more money working for myself and being an employee was now holding me back. They fired me right before Christmas and allowed me to finally invest all my time in my business. This gave me the gift of taking the same leap of faith every entrepreneur must take to thrive instead of just surviving.

CRAFTING THE VISION

If I've learned anything, it's that clarity comes from vision. And vision doesn't come from hustle, productivity planners or podcasts. It comes from God. But here's the catch: you can't *hear* the vision if you're drowning in noise. That's why Jesus went to the wilderness. Not because he was lost—but because that is where he was tested and proven. Jesus remained faithful and obedient to God overcoming temptation. His forty days of fasting, prayer, and solitude with God prepared him for public ministry. He needed to *endure*. And so do we. If your spirit is overstimulated, distracted, or addicted to the next notification, you won't have a connection to God. You'll miss the breadcrumbs and walk right past your assignment. I did multiple times, but God thankfully kept on redirecting me.

The first step is to tune in by getting into a positive environment even if you don't know anyone there. God doesn't stop talking; it's just that most of us aren't listening. Messages come in nudges, patterns, synchronizations, gut feelings, dreams, coincidences, and even pain. But they won't register if you're numbed out or in tune to the wrong frequency, which has everything to do with your surroundings. You must remember that all losses have meaning the same way that all failures have lessons. It is your choice to learn it once and move forward, or to keep having the same lesson presented over and over until you do. The only way failure becomes permanent is when *you* let it by choosing to give up.

Looking back, every major turning point in my life came after I got still and created space to listen and submit. Vision is divine; it plugs you in to something bigger, and once it's clear, your life becomes a response to it.

Submission is when you say, "I'm not just following the plan, I'm surrendering to the outcome." It's when you let go of how *you* think it's supposed to go and trust the vision God gave you, even when it leads somewhere unexpected, inconvenient, or painful. Pain is temporary, but God's love is forever. You must trust him and remain faithful just as Jesus did for all of us. You see, commitment is good, but submission is better. Commitment says, "I will." Submission says, "*Your* will."

HELPERS ALONG THE WAY

If vision is the spark, then people are the kindling. Once I submitted to the vision, I started noticing something miraculous: God didn't just send clarity—He sent *company*. Teachers. Helpers. Assignments. The right people, at the right time, with exactly what I needed to learn, receive, or give. He also got rid of toxic people who would not allow me to get to the next level, and He will do the same for you.

Because your life and its purpose are already predetermined by God, you have nothing to worry about, and to do so is a lack of faith. If He gives you the vision, He will give you the tools to obtain victory, and all the glory should go to him for it. This process is unique to everyone, so be grateful for everything that happens to you and know that everything works out in the end. All those breadcrumbs will amount to a beautiful loaf of bread created specifically for you!

About Michael

Michael has been in the storm restoration industry for fifteen years and is an expert on the insurance-claims process. His unique background, working for and now against the insurance companies, has allowed him to serve his clients at the highest level. His experience as a contractor has also played an imperative role in refining his skill set for negotiating scopes of work on behalf of his customers because experience matters.

Michael started as an independent adjuster for Cunningham Lindsey for four years, adjusting claims all over the country for insurance companies while finishing his MBA at Our Lady of the Lake University in San Antonio. It was during this time that he started his first business in secret as a general contractor specializing in roofing. His vision was to take the business from its humble beginnings out of the trunk of his car to the full-time business it would become, allowing him out of his role as an employee. Michael now works directly for policyholders needing help getting paid what they are rightfully owed for their residential or commercial insurance losses.

Mike is passionate about educating and advocating his customers through the complex claims process to make them whole again. Michael now consults other public adjusters and contractors with the vision of helping to unite this side of the industry because it is in the best interests of the policyholders, considering that the other side of the industry is already united against them, for the most part.

Michael is a loving husband to his wife, Natali, and devoted father to Eli and Allia. He spends as much time as possible with his family. They are one of the driving forces for his relentless work ethic and his greatest gifts from God. Michael loves travel, good food, live music, and reading, which are all passions he shares with his family.

Follow Michael on IG @MikeAcerra and learn more:
www.mikeathepa.com
www.mikeacerra.com

CHAPTER 6

ROCK-BOTTOM REBOOT

The Power of a Personal Audit

By Deanna Sullivan

"Your position is being terminated, effective immediately."

Just like that. No warning. One minute I was a global partner at the most prestigious accounting firm in the world. The next, I was unemployed. My office? Cleared out. My stake in the partnership? Forfeited. In the fall of 2001 things started happening at Enron and the SEC began investigating my firm. Some employees shredded documents related to Enron and the SEC indicted us for obstruction of justice in March 2002. We were found guilty in July 2002 and officially surrendered our CPA license in August. Later, the Supreme Court would overturn the conviction, but it would be too late.

I hung up the phone that day totally numb. A scandal I had nothing to do with turned my life upside down. I thought I'd hit rock bottom and called my husband, needing to hear his voice and encouragement. "I think we should get a divorce," he said.

What followed was an avalanche of loss and heartbreak. I was still grieving the death of my mother. My marriage was officially over. My grandmother passed away. While I was on a trip, my home was burglarized and emptied of precious memories. My career was obliterated. It was one storm after another. And my sweet father, trying to comfort me, said what no one else had the courage to say out loud: "Gee, Deanna, you worked so hard. And now you have nothing." He was right. At least it felt that way.

No title. No office. No team. No husband. No "success," as I had always defined it. I'd spent a lifetime chasing gold stars in the form of degrees, promotions, houses, and in the blink of an eye, it all vanished.

I was at rock bottom. But rock bottom has a strange gift buried inside it: clarity. I had made a career out of auditing organizations – analyzing processes, assessing risks and controls, testing for alignment with goals and objectives. The result - what's working, what's not, and opportunities for improvement. Eventually, I realized I needed to do the same thing with my life. I had to take a hard, honest look at my own internal systems— my beliefs, my priorities, my definition of success. I had to ask myself the same questions I used to ask my clients: What's really adding value? What's no longer sustainable? That personal audit changed everything.

What I discovered in the aftermath wasn't how to reclaim my old life, but how to redefine success entirely and how to train my mind not just to survive, but to use new principles of growth to build something even more meaningful than before. Today, I use these same principles to coach my clients and the data is conclusive: you can't manage what you don't measure, and you can't measure what you don't know. The audit is key.

REINVENTION

My pastor once said, *"Success is doing God's will for your life."* I believe that. Real success is about taking the gifts God gave you and using them to make a difference in someone else's life.

I used to think success was measured in promotions, paychecks, and possessions. Now I know that's just accumulation. What I'm after now is *significance*. Today, I lead SullivanSolutions, where I help businesses stay ethically grounded and protect themselves from fraud through transformational education and workshops. But more than that, I help people think differently. I encourage them to ask three simple, powerful questions—Who do I want to be? What do I want to do? What do I want to have? Always in that order. This was my big step out of rock bottom.

After the firm imploded and my marriage dissolved, I had to ask the one question no one wants to ask: *Who am I now?* For the first time in my adult life, I had a blank slate. And that's both terrifying and liberating. I reflected. I talked to recruiters and coaches. I explored coaching, motivational speaking, even being a golf club rep—until I realized you practically had to be Tiger Woods to do that. Then, a friend called and asked if I'd be willing to teach for her organization on a contract basis. I said yes. That "yes" was the spark. I discovered I had a knack for making auditing and ethics not only understandable, but entertaining. I found joy in educating and that opportunity gave me the runway to eventually launch my own business. I was no longer looking at rock bottom.

I never thought I'd be an entrepreneur. I had always worked within an organization. But when I realized the heart of entrepreneurship was *helping people,* I leaned in. Reinvention is not just about fixing what's broken. It's about aligning your gifts with your purpose and having the courage to pivot when the old way no longer fits. If you're standing in the rubble of something that used to define you—your job, your marriage, your identity—I'm here to tell you: it's not the end. It's the invitation to climb out of rock bottom.

You *can* start over. You *can* build a new life. A personal audit is not meant to simply spotlight your vulnerabilities, but to reveal new opportunities for growth and alignment. There are no right or wrong answers. It's all information you can use to step forward into the next phase of your success with clarity and confidence.

MINDSET

If reinvention is the decision to start again, *mindset* is what keeps you going when the road gets bumpy. When the rug was pulled out from under my feet, I was tempted to take the practical path, revamp my resume and find another job. But deep down, I knew I'd be settling. I had to trust that God had given me gifts for a reason. My faith has been my anchor, my compass, and my fuel. It's what kept me steady in the storm. And faith and mindset are inextricably linked.

You see, your mindset will be your engine that powers you forward—or your anchor that pulls you down. And like Zig Ziglar used to say, "You've got to get rid of the stinkin' thinkin'!"

It all comes down to persistence. It's the daily decision to believe that your dreams are worth the effort and that your "why" is strong enough to outlast your challenges. If you don't know *why*, the "how" will wear you down. That's why I keep a vision board on my wall. Not to manifest a new car, but to remind me of my values and to keep my eyes on the dream, the mission, and the legacy I want to leave behind.

Your mindset is either lifting you up—or locking you down.

ALIGNMENT

What matters so much to you that you'd walk across the sky for it? I often teach this lesson and every time I do, it stops people in their tracks. I ask the group, "How many of you have children under the age of six?" Hands shoot up. Then I say, "Now imagine we have an I-beam on the floor—a big steel girder—about 8 inches tall off the ground, like a balance beam. Could you walk across it?" Of course, everyone nods. Easy enough. Then I raise the stakes.

"Now imagine we've magically stretched that same I-beam across the top of the Petronas Towers in Kuala Lumpur—spire to spire, hundreds of feet in the air. No harness. No safety net. Would you walk across it now?" The room goes quiet.

Most people say what you're probably thinking: Absolutely not. It's not worth the risk.

So, I say, "Okay, let's raise the stakes again. I'll give you a million dollars if you walk across." A few people consider it, but even then, most realize that money isn't worth risking death. Then I say, "Now imagine your child is on the other tower and must be saved. The only way to reach them is that I-beam." Without hesitation, everyone says they'd walk across.

That is alignment. When you know what matters most, your decisions get crystal clear. Now, not all values are I-beam worthy. You won't walk across for a bonus or a title. But you will for your child, your faith, your purpose. The question becomes: What's worth walking the I-beam?

Are you living for things you wouldn't even risk a scrape for, let alone your life? People *say* their values are family, faith, freedom, but then spend every waking hour at the office, missing birthdays and burning out for a job they secretly resent. Or they *say* they value adventure and travel, but they're stuck in a role that's killing their spirit. If your calendar, your career, and your conversations don't reflect what you *say* you value, you're out of alignment. Ethics aren't just about right or wrong. They're about making decisions that reflect your values.

Early in my career, I had a choice. I was working on a major oil and gas project with a world-class consulting firm when I was offered an internal audit position that would require a move to Dallas. It wasn't a promotion. The path wasn't clear. But my *gut* told me it was right. It aligned with what I wanted: exposure to the entire business and the chance to travel the world.

So, I took the leap, and it was one of the best decisions of my life. I fell in love with the internal audit profession, made lifelong connections and saw the world!

If you're facing a big decision, here's what I recommend: Make a list of the pros and cons. Then ask yourself, "Does this align with who I am and who I want to be?" Sometimes your gut will tell you to go against the "smart" choice. Listen. Because as a leader, your values aren't just personal, they're *directional*.

Remember: success is hollow if it costs you alignment. And you can't build a phenomenal life walking someone else's path. The next time you're standing at the edge of a decision, ask yourself: *Would I cross the I-beam for this?* If the answer is no, it's not worth your time. If it's yes, walk with purpose.

ADAPTABILITY

In 2008, when the economy tanked, so did my consulting business. Overnight, my phone stopped ringing. When companies need to make cuts, training and development are the first things to go. Now, I *knew* the old saying, "Don't put all your eggs in one basket," but I had a fabulous client who kept me busy with steady work. That client had all my eggs! Never wait for a storm to figure out how to build a boat. I realized if I wanted to survive, I had to adapt. So, I asked myself, "What do organizations need no matter what the economy is doing?"

They need to be ethically sound.

A friend suggested I become certified to teach ethics to Texas CPAs. CPAs are required to take ethics training to keep their license. So are Certified Internal Auditors and Certified Fraud Examiners. I did the research, developed a course, and submitted it to the Texas State Board. That ethics course has been one of my most successful offerings for over 14 years. Has it been easy? No. It takes constant updating, new case studies, evolving regulations, and fresh fraud stories (which, unfortunately, are never in short supply). But it gave me new ways to serve. And best of all, it aligned with my mission to help people and businesses do the right thing.

Here's what I learned, and what I hope you'll take with you:

- Diversify your offerings. One product or one client isn't a business—it's a dependency.
- Research what people actually need and build your skills to meet that need.
- Embrace change. Don't resist it. Don't fear it. *Use* it.
- And don't put all your eggs in one basket!

If you want a fun, fast reminder of why adaptability matters, go read *Who Moved My Cheese?* by Spencer Johnson. It's a simple parable, but the wisdom is deep. The lesson is that if you don't change, you can become extinct. Success doesn't come to the smartest or the strongest but to those who are adaptable, flexible and willing to move when the cheese moves.

Learn to bend without breaking and to adapt without abandoning your values. Because the world *will* change. The question is… will you change with it?

SERVICE

John Maxwell says, "Leadership is influence." Real leaders don't manage, they *serve*.

Towards the end of my time at the firm, one of the most powerful ways I led was by helping my team get what *they* wanted. For some, that meant less travel. For others, it was high visibility. I did my best to deliver because when people feel valued, they show up differently. They give more, care more and the team wins. Contrast that with my early days as a supervisor in oil and gas. Back then, I thought leadership meant making sure people came back from lunch on time. I had no clue what *they* wanted in life. I was managing hours, not outcomes.

I've since learned that true leadership is about *empowering* people, not micromanaging them. Two of my favorite tools to use are DISC and BrainStyles. These behavior assessment tools give us insight into how we make decisions, how we process information, and how we learn and communicate. Once we understand each other's wiring, the friction fades, and the collaboration soars. And that's what service is all about: understanding others so you can meet them where they are.

Leadership is not about flaunting credentials, managing time sheets and exploiting the built-in power differential. It's about caring. As Zig used to say, "People don't care how much you know until they know how much you care, about them."

PURPOSE

I've been surrounded by success in every worldly form, but the greatest success I've known didn't come with a paycheck. It came from doing a courageous audit on my life.

When everything fell apart—my firm, my marriage, my identity—I had to ask myself the hard questions I used to ask companies: What's working? What's out of alignment? What's adding value? What needs to go? And when I ran that audit, I realized success isn't about what you accumulate. It's about whether your life reflects what you say you value.

My dad was never rich, but he lived a life of purpose and principle. He loved people, served others and stuck to his word. In the end, he was deeply respected. That's the kind of balance sheet I hope to have. My advice? Audit your life. Ask yourself if your choices line up with your values. Ask if your success is just impressive, or deeply meaningful. And ask, most of all, "What legacy do I want to leave?"

In the end what will matter is not what you earned or owned but how you lived and who you served.

About Deanna

Deanna Sullivan is an internationally recognized speaker, author, and trainer on a mission to make education not only effective but genuinely enjoyable. With every session, she brings a dynamic blend of insight, humor, and inspiration to help audiences achieve their personal and professional goals.

A sought-after keynote speaker and facilitator, Deanna has captivated audiences across the globe, with appearances in cities including Dubai, Copenhagen, Sydney, Shanghai, Geneva, Rome, Toronto, Vancouver, Mexico City, London, Amsterdam, Stockholm, Helsinki, Oslo, Sofia, Istanbul, Johannesburg, Jakarta, Hong Kong, and Kuala Lumpur. She leads programs in both technical and leadership development, with signature topics covering fraud prevention, ethics, communication, and personal effectiveness.

Deanna is certified to teach ethics for Texas CPAs and is often praised for her ability to make the topic refreshingly engaging—earning feedback such as, "The best ethics course I've ever attended!" She is also a proud Ziglar Legacy Trainer, sharing the enduring wisdom of her hero, Zig Ziglar, around the world. In addition, Deanna is a DISC Certified Trainer, using behavioral insights to help individuals and teams enhance communication and performance. And as a member of the Maxwell Leadership Certified Team, Deanna incorporates John Maxwell's undeniable laws of leadership and growth to enrich participants' experiences even further.

Her passion for uplifting others extends into her personal life as well—Deanna teaches Bible study at Second Baptist Church and volunteers as a speaker for the Houston Livestock Show and Rodeo, inspiring students and professionals alike.

As the founder and principal of SullivanSolutions, Deanna helps organizations and individuals improve performance through tailored training and consulting services. With a background spanning auditing, accounting, and global risk consulting, including her role as global director of process and methodology for Arthur Andersen's Risk Consulting Practice, Deanna brings both heart and depth to everything she does.

Learn more at SullivanSolutions.net.

CHAPTER 7

IT'S NEVER TOO LATE

How Failure Forged My Future

By Michael Killen

The cold cut through to my bones, but it wasn't the steel bench I sat on or the cinder-block walls pressing in from all sides.

This cold was deeper—the kind that settles into your bones when you realize you've hit bottom. I looked toward the window. Somewhere beyond the concrete and barbed wire, it was a bright winter morning, but I wouldn't feel the warmth of the sun—because I was morally bankrupt, physically wrecked, spiritually dead, sitting in a jail cell in bewilderment and disbelief.

Nobody ever plans for this. Nobody ever thinks they'll end up here. And yet here I was.

The Bible says, "Every man's way is right in his own eyes, but the Lord weighs the heart." (Proverbs 21:2, NASB). I had spent years justifying the wreckage I left behind—the lies, the broken promises—telling myself I wasn't that bad. But when you wake up behind bars, you can't lie to yourself anymore.

My father had sent me a copy of the Big Book of AA, and for the first time in my life, I was trying to reach for something bigger than myself, trying to find God in that dark, stale cell.

And then, on that winter morning, something happened. I looked out the tiny scratched window, and in an instant I felt a weight lift out of me. The pull that had owned me, that craving that twisted inside me for years, was simply gone. Physically gone. Spiritually gone. For the first time since I could remember, I didn't ache to be out there chasing the next high. I didn't feel pulled toward chaos, temptation, or destruction. I felt free, truly free. It wasn't the kind of freedom a judge could grant. It was the kind of freedom that only God can give. I said a simple prayer that day: "God, if you can use what I've been through to help somebody else, then so be it."

That was the day I woke up not just sober—but *alive*.

But the real test came after the cell doors opened, when I had to step back into the world and trust that faith would lead me forward.

FORGED IN FAITH

Most people think AA is just about quitting drinking. It's not. It's about living by a new code—one rooted in humility, surrender, and faith in a power greater than yourself. It's about doing the next right thing, even when no one is watching and staying the course of integrity.

I would need that code to weather everything that came next.

After I got out on work release, a man took a chance on me—or so I thought. He was hiring guys straight out of jail because it was cheap labor, plain and simple. But I didn't care. I was on fire for life! I built his website, learned about his business, and did everything I could to add value.

One day he told me he had been an attorney before, and the stories he shared raised a few red flags. For three years I watched and listened, eventually realizing that I was working for a man who had once profited off other people's misfortune and was still making up stories and living without integrity. And that's where the seed for my own business was planted. I thought, "What if we took the same business model but actually treated people right? What if we followed through on our promises? What if we built something on truth instead of manipulation?"

I decided to leave and start my own company, Amish Yard, selling high-quality outdoor furniture with old-school values. My former boss didn't take it well. He sued me. Over and over.

Frivolous lawsuits over things as ridiculous as a borrowed animal cage he says I never returned. Then, he took it a step further, sending a letter to the Amish community, the very people I was building relationships with, claiming I had relapsed and was back on drugs. It was a lie.

I have never relapsed. It cut deep because when you build your life on redemption, it doesn't just hurt when people lie about you; it feels as if they're trying to erase what you bled to build. The truth came out—it always does—but it wasn't easy, and maybe that's why I'm so grateful for it. I kept doing the next right thing. I kept showing up, telling the truth, and keeping my word. And little by little we grew.

Amish Yard didn't just survive; it thrived. Our success wasn't accidental. It was the result of a few timeless principles, forged in failure and refined through faith, that shaped every decision, setback, and breakthrough that followed. These principles became the foundation for lasting growth—not just in business but in character, leadership, and life itself. Try them for yourself.

TAKE OFF YOUR HAT

In those early years I thought leadership meant carrying everything on my own back.

I believed that if I wanted something done right, I had to do it myself. At first, it seemed like a badge of honor—the long hours, the endless problem-solving, the constant pressure. But over time, I realized I was unintentionally limiting the growth of everyone around me. I wasn't leading; I was bottlenecking.

By doing everything myself, I wasn't just burning myself out, I was robbing my team of the opportunity to rise, take ownership, and discover what they were capable of. When you cling too tightly to control, you don't just slow your own progress; you stunt the development of everyone who depends on you.

It took time—and a lot of humility—to shift that mindset. Letting go felt risky. Delegating felt uncomfortable. But real leadership isn't about being the one who knows or does everything; it's about being the one who builds others up to stand strong on their own.

Today, everything is different. Now, I invest in my people and bring the entire team to conferences, workshops, and events not just so they can grow into their roles, but so they can eventually *outgrow* them. Because true leadership isn't measured by how much you can personally achieve; it's measured by how many lives you can impact beyond your own. If you find yourself stuck in the trap of doing everything yourself, ask yourself this: "What am I holding on to that someone else could grow through?" One of the measures of a great leader is how willing they are to let go so others can step in and soar.

GO BACK TO GO FORWARD

Sometimes growth doesn't come from pushing forward. It comes from stepping back and seeing things differently. For years, our primary location had felt like home. Even though it was a month-to-month lease, the landowners had made it clear they had no plans to sell, and we trusted that. Then, out of nowhere, everything changed. The landlord called and told us a hospital had made an offer on the property, and they were taking it. We had thirty days to vacate. Thirty days to uproot everything we had built.

I was stunned. The weight of it hit me so hard I had to lay down on the floor and just breathe. When the pressure builds that fast, sometimes you have to step away and find a different perspective. I booked a flight to Florida, where my mentor, Howard, was leading a conference, and we spent the day together, walking along the water. At one point, Howard picked up a rock and placed it in the sand. He told me to stand there and jump as far as I could. He marked the spot where I landed and said, "Now, take a few steps back, get a running start, and jump again." This time, I flew three times farther. He smiled and said something so simple but so wise it has stayed with me ever since: "Sometimes you have to go back before you can go forward."

When I got home, I realized I needed a plan, not just a reaction. The hospital needed us out quickly, and that gave me leverage. On a coaching call with Howard, I told him I was thinking about asking the hospital to give us $15,000 to help with the sudden move. He paused, then asked me how much I thought the hospital's project was worth. I didn't know, but I figured it was millions. "And you're going to ask for fifteen thousand?" he asked, raising an eyebrow.

I renegotiated and ended up securing $105,000 to help with the transition — seven times more than I would have ever dared to ask on my own. Sometimes life knocks you backward not to punish you, but to set you up for a greater leap. Every obstacle hides an opportunity if you're willing to stop, step back, and see it.

The truth is, I wouldn't have seen that opportunity—let alone had the courage to seize it—without someone wiser standing in my corner. If there's one thing I've learned, it's that growth rarely happens alone. Behind every breakthrough in my life, there's been a mentor who helped me see farther, think bigger, and believe deeper than I could on my own.

WHO IS IN YOUR CORNER?

Looking back, one of the most pivotal decisions I ever made was choosing to get help.

It wasn't easy at first. After years of doing everything myself, it was hard to admit I didn't have all the answers, but I had come to a point where I couldn't deny it any longer.

We were ten years into the business and expecting our son, Ryder. I wanted to slow down and be present with my family and thought I'd built something strong enough to stand without me. Yet when I stepped back, everything started to fall apart. I was scrambling for answers, signing up for college courses, searching for anything that would help me get back on track. It was during that time of uncertainty that I had met Howard.

At the time, hiring him felt like a leap of faith. It was a significant investment, and I wasn't sure I could justify it. But he told me, "They won't teach you what you need to know in college. I will." Something in me knew he was right. I didn't need more textbooks or theories. I needed real-world wisdom from someone who had walked the path and could show me the way.

Looking back now, it's easy to see how fruitful that decision was. Howard didn't just help me rebuild the business. He taught me how to lead it differently, take bolder steps, and trust in my ability to build something that could thrive. The relationship was worth every penny—and then some.

After we had worked together for some time, Howard flew in to spend a day with me, and I wanted to show him the best of what Pittsburgh had to offer. I took him to a beautiful restaurant perched high on Mount Washington, the kind of place where you can see the entire city laid out beneath you. We had an incredible meal, talking about business, leadership, and life.

After dinner, we gazed out the window, taking in the breathtaking view. It was a moment that felt almost surreal, sitting there, the owner of a thriving company, with the mentor who had helped me get there. And then, I spotted it: the county jail. I stood there looking at the same place where, years earlier, I had woken up broken, lost, and hopeless.

Howard noticed I had gotten quiet and asked what I was looking at. I was reluctant to tell him about my past but once I did, his face lit up! He affirmed how far I had come and told me that someday my story would help countless others. It was a beautiful full-circle moment and a reminder of how far God had carried me. None of it would have been possible without the willingness to admit I needed help, the courage to seek out mentorship, and the faith to believe that with the right guidance, even the most broken beginnings could lead to a life of purpose, success, and meaning.

BUILDING A POWERFUL FUTURE

Today, success for me doesn't just hinge on sales and revenue. While those things still matter, they're not the measure of my life. In addition to running my company, I spend time helping others attain and maintain sobriety.

Some of my greatest joy comes from coaching. I coach adults who are on a sober journey, and I coach my kids' sports teams. And it's funny how many parallels there are between coaching and leading a business. Leadership is leadership, whether you're managing a sales team or a group of third-graders with grass-stained knees.

I often reflect on the man I was—the one who woke up in a jail cell, lost and hopeless, convinced he had ruined any chance at a good life. And now, when I look back, I feel nothing but love for that version of me. He was doing the best he could with what he knew.

I wouldn't change a thing. Because today, by the grace of God, I have a family that inspires me, a business that makes a difference, and—most importantly—a life filled with purpose. My son said something recently that struck me right between the eyes. We were rushing to get out the door, and I got frustrated and said, "It's too late." He looked up at me and said, "It's never too late." And he's right.

It's never too late to change, to grow, and to become the person you were meant to be.

No matter how far you've fallen, no matter how hopeless it feels, no matter what you think you've lost—it's never too late. Today, my goal is simple: to be of maximum service, to fulfill whatever potential I've been given, and to ask each day for the strength to do God's will and the courage to carry it out.

You don't have to have a perfect past to build a powerful future. No story is too far gone for God to rewrite. If God can rebuild a life as broken as mine, He can rebuild anything. True success is when your life becomes living proof that grace is real, redemption is possible, and your deepest failures can fuel your greatest purpose.

About Michael

Michael Killen is the founder of Amish Yard LLC, an award-winning company that has grown over the years to serve customers with quality outdoor products and a focus on honest, dependable service. What began as a small venture—with a $10,000 loan from his father—has steadily developed into a successful business, thanks to hard work, persistence, and support from others along the way.

With more than twenty years of experience in the industry, Michael's journey has been shaped by a desire to keep learning and improving. He's a Certified Human Behavior Consultant with a focus on the DISC model, and he tries to bring those insights into how he works with others and approaches daily life. Influenced by the Ziglar philosophy, Michael values positive thinking, humility, and steady personal growth.

At home Michael is a husband to Ashlee and a proud father to Ryder and Jessie. He treasures the time he spends coaching their sports teams and being present in their lives. Fitness and faith are also important parts of his routine, helping him stay grounded and balanced.

Michael cares deeply about his local community and feels fortunate to be in a position where he can give back—whether that's helping someone grow a business or offering support to those on a path to recovery. He doesn't see himself as having all the answers, but he's always willing to walk alongside others and lend a hand when he can.

He and his family live in South Park, Pennsylvania, where they enjoy the simple things—spending time together, staying active, and being part of the local community. It's there that Michael finds balance between his personal and professional life, drawing inspiration from the people and values that surround him.

Michael's story is one of learning, gratitude, and service. He continues to grow as a business owner, father, and friend, committed to his faith and to inspiring others to grow in theirs.

Learn more:

MichaelJKillen.com
AmishYard.com

CHAPTER 8

CRAFTING A LEGACY THROUGH FAITH

By Nick and Jamie Hallas

I can still remember the day I felt the nudge from God. My stomach was in knots over a project my boss had just handed to me. He wanted me to cut corners and do something that went against the National Electrical Code—and against my values.

I called my wife Jamie and said, "I think it's time. God is giving the green light."

For months we had prayed for clarity about when to step out on our own. Sitting there on that job site, I knew this was it. When I gave my two weeks' notice, they didn't take it well. They fired me on the spot instead of letting me finish out the time. One day I was employed, the next we were fully on our own with four kids to feed, a mortgage to pay, and no guarantees in front of us.

By God's grace, we got our first job right away, a confirmation that we hadn't imagined His leading. But the early days were tight. The jobs came slowly. The savings account started dwindling, and it wasn't long before fear came knocking.

One Sunday after service, a kind lady from church told Jamie there was a job opening at Harley-Davidson, good pay, good benefits, all the security that looked pretty appealing in that moment. Jamie wanted me to apply. She saw the mounting bills and was understandably scared. Honestly, I was scared too, and I was ready to apply just to put our minds at ease; but that's when faith tapped Jamie on the shoulder.

She remembered all the nights we had prayed, all the confirmations that this wasn't just a good idea — it was *God's* idea. She realized that by asking me to go back to the familiar, she was putting her fear above our faith. And right there, we came to a decision that shaped everything that came after. We decided we weren't going to chase comfort. We were going to chase *calling*.

Choosing faith didn't make the fear vanish or magically multiply the dollars in the bank account. But it shifted the weight. We stopped carrying the burden by ourselves and handed it back to the One who had called us to this vision in the first place.

Looking back now, it's so clear. We didn't just start a business; we started a journey of trusting God in ways we never had before. That first year didn't turn around overnight. Growth was slow. We had four kids then (and six now), and some days we didn't know how the next bill was going to get paid. At the time, we couldn't wait for the hard days to end. Now, we wouldn't trade them for anything. Those tight days, those tough lessons, the nights in fervent prayer, were the training ground where God grew us into people who could actually carry the blessing He had for us.

If you find yourself standing at the edge of something bigger than you, scared and tempted to turn back, we want you to know it's okay to be scared. But don't let fear drive the bus. Security might seem easier in the moment, but nothing will ever compare to the steady peace that comes from knowing you're right where God wants you to be. God doesn't call the equipped. He equips the called. And if He called you, He *will* provide.

Looking back, we can see there were a few key lessons — factors of faith — that made all the difference between giving up and growing a business that changes lives.

FACTOR 1: GATHER THE KNOWLEDGE

When we first stepped out on our own, we had a lot of grit, prayer, and a whole lot of determination. What we didn't have was a system, a process or the kind of business knowledge that helps you work smarter instead of harder.

Nick was doing everything he knew how to do—working sunup to sundown, taking every job he could get, just to keep us afloat. And I felt helpless. I didn't know anything about business and didn't feel qualified to help him in the ways he needed it most. I just knew he was burning himself out, and I didn't want him to carry the whole load alone.

We realized that if we were going to build something that lasted, we were going to have to grow ourselves. That's when God opened the next door.

We heard about a conference being put on by Howard Partridge, and even though the thought of going to a business conference made me more than a little uncomfortable, we went. I'll never forget sitting there, hearing story after story of small business owners who had been exactly where we were—exhausted, overwhelmed, and one decision away from either breakthrough or burnout. It lit a fire in me! After that conference, we got plugged into a weekly coaching group. Every week we'd call in, and I'd listen, lurking in the background while holding the baby. Week after week I started learning—not everything all at once, but enough to see where I could finally start helping. I soon gained enough confidence to join Nick on the calls. I went through what is called "financial blast"—kind of a bookkeeping boot camp— and slowly but surely, we started putting real systems in place.

I went from feeling like "just a stay-at-home mom," scared to even sit in on a business meeting, to someone who could schedule precious time with our kids *and* still help move our business forward. I even started leading some of our team meetings. The truth is, faith without knowledge is a wish, not a plan. And God doesn't call us to wish. He calls us to *work*—to gather the tools and the wisdom we'll need to carry out the calling He's given us. Gathering the right knowledge was the foundation we didn't even realize we were missing. And once we had it, faith had something solid to stand on.

Factor 2: Consistently Showing Up

When we look back, one of the biggest reasons we're still standing today—as a business and as a family—is because we made a key decision early on: We would keep showing up no matter what.

It sounds simple, but when you're tired, scared, and wondering if you made the biggest mistake of your life, it's not simple at all. There were days when everything in us wanted to crawl under the covers and not come out. If we had a disagreement, if home-schooling felt like too much, if the paperwork piled up and the lawyer kept calling, the last thing we felt like doing was showing up to another business meeting.

One night, as I laid there overwhelmed and exhausted, I heard it so clearly in my spirit: "Keep showing up." Not "do it perfectly." Not "have it all figured out." Just "Keep Showing Up."

When you're walking by faith, you can't make decisions based on your mood. You have to keep putting one foot in front of the other, not because you feel like it, but because you remember what you're walking toward.

Success—in business, in marriage, in anything—doesn't come from doing the easy things when you're motivated. It comes from doing the right things even when you're tired, scared, or unsure. We realized that showing up wasn't about how we felt in the moment. It was about the promises God had spoken over our lives and the calling He had placed in our hands. You don't build anything that lasts by chasing feelings. You build it by choosing faith over fear and commitment over comfort. When you consistently show up in faith, God consistently shows up with provision, strength, and wisdom. It's not always overnight, but it's always on time.

Factor 3: Ask for Guidance

When you're stepping into new territory, one of the smartest things you can do is find someone who's already been where you're trying to go.

As our business grew, we hired more employees, and doubled in size practically overnight. On the outside, that sounds like success—and it was—but inside, it felt overwhelming. We weren't just doing more work. We had new challenges, a bigger team, a new culture to build, systems to rework, and the pressure of knowing that more people were counting on us than before. We needed help. We needed to get around people who had been where we were and could show us the way forward.

When we found out about the conference being hosted by Howard, it would have been easy to say, "We don't have time for this," or "We can't afford it right now;" but standing there at the end of the first conference, after hearing about leadership, systems, marketing, sales, administration, and the DISC model, Nick said something that became a defining moment: "If we don't do this, I might as well go get a job."

Once again, we were faced with the same question we'd faced so many times before: Would we trust God and move forward, or would we retreat back to comfort because it was easier to explain? We joined the coaching program. Looking back now, it's impossible to even put into words what that decision meant for our family, our business, and our future. Through that community, we learned how to finally get our financial controls in order. We learned how to build systems (and we're still building them!), how to lead people better, how to use our time more wisely, how to market, how to sell, and maybe most importantly, how to believe in the gifts God had already placed inside us.

But beyond that, we learned through being around other business owners with similar goals, that success isn't about being perfect. It's about being willing to keep learning, being humble enough to ask questions and being wise enough to get around people who won't just tell you what you want to hear but will share what you *need* to hear. Gathering knowledge is important, but having solid mentors and trusted colleagues on speed dial is absolutely vital to success. For us, success has rested on both skilling up and reaching out!

When we look back on our journey, we can say without a doubt that we didn't get here alone. We got here because we listened, we learned, and we leaned on the teachers God sent our way.

Factor 4: Growth Is Not Linear

Like many business owners, when we first started out, we thought growth would look like a straight line—steady, upward, always forward. Turns out, real growth looks a whole lot more like swimming toward a boat you can barely see that keeps moving farther and farther away from you.

Not long ago we purchased our competitor and quickly realized that big steps stir up big waves. There were days we felt like we were barely breaking the surface long enough to gasp for air before getting dragged back under.

This season has been one of the toughest in both our business and our personal life. There have been moments when we questioned whether we made the right decision or had reached too far. And yet, every time we stop and pray, every time we look back on our journey, we can see God's hand was in it all along.

One of the Scriptures that has carried us through this time is: "The steps of a good man are ordered by the Lord, and he delighteth in his way. Though he fall, he shall not be utterly cast down: for the Lord upholdeth him with His hand" (Psalm 37:23–24). Growth is not about getting everything right the first time. It's about trusting that God is ordering your steps, even when it feels like you're falling.

Factor 5: Faith and Family First

From the beginning, we knew we wanted to build more than a business. We wanted to build strong families, starting with our own.

We've seen firsthand how important it is to keep faith and family at the center of everything. And it's not just words on a mission statement. It's the decisions we make, day after day, even when it's hard.

We once hired a man who had worked in a big city for years. He had come to Northern Wisconsin looking for his retirement home. He couldn't find a job at first, so we offered him one. In his old job, he was just a number. Here, he's part of a family. He told us recently that what we gave him wasn't just work, it was the chance to finally live the life he had dreamed about for his family. That's what building a strong business really means to us.

We don't chase every opportunity that comes our way. We choose work that keeps us rooted here, close to home. If it's a high-paying job out of town that would pull us away for long stretches, we turn it down. Because no paycheck is worth losing sight of the mission. When one of our team members, a veteran, struggled with sleep and couldn't always show up on time, we didn't just throw him away. We listened and practiced empathy. We worked with him because we believe people are more than their performance on their worst days.

Our mission is clear: Build strong families. Start with our own. Then help others do the same. If we can keep that order right—faith, family, business—we know we'll be right where God wants us to be.

KEEP STEPPING FORWARD

If there's one thing we've learned through all of this, it's that success in business, marriage, faith and life isn't a walk in the park!

There are moments it feels like you've fallen right off a cliff! But if you stay faithful—if you keep learning, showing up, and doing the next right thing—you start to see a pattern emerge.

Nick always says it like this: "If you can step back from the picture—even if you feel like you've fallen off the graph—you'll see that the long-term trajectory is still up." It's just like the stock market. There are dips, crashes and days that feel like total failure. But zoom out far enough, and you realize the line is still rising.

It's the same with walking by faith. God doesn't promise us a smooth ride, but He does promise that He's ordering our steps, even when they feel shaky. And He promises that if we trust Him, He will make our paths fruitful even if they take a few detours along the way.

For us, this journey hasn't just been about building a business. It's been about building a life that reflects what we believe—that faith comes first, family is sacred, and success is measured not just in the money we make but in the lives we touch and the legacy we leave.

About Nick and Jamie

Nick and Jamie are the powerhouses behind ICT Electric, a flourishing electrical business in the Northwoods of Wisconsin. Since marrying in 2003, they have fused their passion for hard work, community, and family into a life of purpose and impact. With their six extraordinary children, they have built a legacy grounded in service, faith, and connection.

Nick's career in the electrical trade began in 2001 with his apprenticeship, where he quickly mastered the craft. He earned his journeyman license in 2006 and his master electrician certification in 2008, reflecting his skill and determination. In 2012 Nick and Jamie launched ICT Electric, which grew into a trusted cornerstone of the Northwoods, powering homes, businesses, and community spaces. Their commitment to quality and community has earned them deep trust and respect.

Jamie is the power driving the company's success by building systems that enhance efficiency and growth. A Ziglar Legacy Certified Trainer and Coach, she draws on Zig Ziglar's principles to inspire others to pursue their goals with purpose. Jamie plays a key role in organizing a sports club for homeschooled children, fostering friendships and character development. Through Howard Partridge's Phenomenal Youth and summer conferences, she empowers the next generation to live with intention and faith.

Together, Nick and Jamie balance entrepreneurship and parenthood with a shared mission to build strong families. Whether wiring or coaching, this duo forges lasting connections that enrich their region. From the spark of electrical work to the warmth of faith-driven leadership, their inspirational journey is one of resilience, purpose, and impact.

To learn more about their electrical business, visit www.incontrolwi. com or call 715-432-1415.

CHAPTER 9

A BLUEPRINT FOR THE MAKING OF A LEADER

By Alyse Makarewicz

I watched her eyes fill with tears as she slowly lowered herself into the seat in front of my desk. As her lips began to quiver, I realized I had done it yet again. I made *another* employee cry. Making people cry seemed to be something I was good at. Not because I was cruel. But because I didn't know any better.

I'd call a team member into my office and march ahead, fast and focused. What I didn't realize was that my energy was intimidating. I'd sit in my office, waiting, and by the time they arrived, they were in tears. Why? Because on that short walk from their desk to mine, they'd constructed an entire narrative of what might be wrong. "What did I do?" "Am I getting fired?"

I didn't see it then, but I was leading through fear, not inspiration. And fear doesn't build trust.

You see, I'm the principal architect and founder of AMB Architects—an HBJ Best Places to Work company and AIA Houston's 2023 Firm of the Year. But that recognition didn't come from my architectural education and experience. It came from intentional growth and transformation—*mine.*

I was six years into building my architectural firm when I entered the Goldman Sachs 10,000 Small Businesses program. I went in looking for a better way to run my business and came out with the awareness that I had a lot of work ahead of me and a better sense of self.

Raw leadership ability, like raw athletic talent, will only get you so far. If you want to become great, you must develop, evolve and mature. Talent might get you in the game, but intentional development is what wins championships.

The world needs more leaders. The only way that happens is if leaders are committed to developing *other* leaders. And there are a few key principles we need to practice to become one of them.

SELF-AWARENESS

Self-awareness is the conscious knowledge of your own character, motives, strengths, weaknesses, and impact on others. It serves as the foundation for authentic and effective leadership.

I used to think I was a great leader because I was driven, focused, and good at getting things done. I wanted to go, go, go and make things happen. What I didn't realize was that my drive created stress for everyone around me. My urgency became their anxiety. I couldn't understand why they weren't keeping up. If I can do it, why can't they? That question used to frustrate me. Now I see it for what it is: a cue to slow down and *look in the mirror.*

When I became aware of the impact I was having, I could finally make the shifts that allowed others around me to thrive. This didn't just show up in my business. It started in my home. My daughter is wired completely differently than I am. I'm a high D on the DISC profile—Dominant and task-oriented. She's an S—Reserved, steady, sensitive, people-oriented. When she was younger, I constantly tried to *fix* her problems. That's my default setting: solve, fix, move forward. She didn't want that. She needed presence, not pressure.

But leadership—in parenting and in business—isn't about being the fixer. It's about building trust by listening before you offer help and direction.. It just so happens that I have many S's as team members and they are less likely to be as straight forward as my daughter. The strategies I have learned from her I've been able to apply in my business. When a challenge occurs, I give my team time to come up with three possible solutions. If it's a reasonable solution, I go with it, even if it was not how I would solve the problem. You can't grow and scale your business if you're the bottleneck and superhero.

The way we're wired isn't wrong, it's just something we have to understand. There's no shame in your default settings, but there *is* power in knowing what they are. You cannot change what you're not aware of. And once you become aware you'll start to notice how often you're operating from default. That realization can be frustrating, but that moment of awareness is a sign you're on the exact path you're supposed to be.

You're not failing. You're evolving.

FEEDBACK IS A GIFT

One of my daily affirmations is this: *Feedback is a gift*. It doesn't always feel like one. In fact, sometimes it feels like being a kid in trouble. But if you can pause, breathe, and receive it, you'll discover something far more valuable than just an opinion. You're given the gift to see out someone else's window and are granted a different perspective. My daughter will sometimes give feedback when she says, "You're yelling at me." I'm not yelling, I'm just talking fast and loud. But that's not how she hears it. I could defend myself or explain my intent. But leadership has taught me to ask a better question: What can I learn from this?

It's the same in architecture. We spend countless hours pouring our creativity into a project, and then someone walks in and starts questioning things or changing our design. That used to trigger me. "You don't have our expertise and experience." I'd want to say, but I've learned that getting defensive cuts off growth. The moment you shut down, you stop listening. And the moment you stop listening, you stop leading. So now I choose to pick the flowers and throw away the weeds.

Feedback doesn't have to be all or nothing. You can take what's useful and release the rest. The beauty of feedback is that it gives you another lens. In creative work, like in leadership, there's rarely just one right answer. Feedback isn't about being right or wrong. It's about being *open*. If you can learn to embrace feedback without shame or shutdown, you'll become a leader who gets better, year after year, because leaders who grow are leaders who *last*.

Know Your Core Values—and Let Them Lead You

I was a vice president at the firm I left before starting AMB Architects. From the outside it seemed like a great company. But on the inside, I started noticing things that didn't sit right with me.

That's when I decided to start my own firm and began developing the foundational culture. I wanted to prove that it was possible to run a successful firm while allowing people—*especially women*—to live full, healthy lives. I believed a forty-hour workweek should be enough and that health insurance, flexibility, and time off weren't luxuries, they were the baseline.

Four years into building AMB, I had my daughter. I wasn't just talking about balance anymore. I was living it and seeing if what I'd built could actually support the life I wanted for myself and for every woman on my team. At first, our values weren't written down, but they were *lived*. Things like efficiency, responsiveness, collaboration, problem solving, and continuous learning—they weren't slogans on the wall, but behaviors we practiced every day. Over time, we put words to what we were already doing. Our culture wasn't built from the top down—it emerged organically, from shared actions and mutual respect. And here's the most powerful part: my team holds *me* accountable to those values.

Your core values aren't just guidelines. They become your compass. Know your core values. Write them down. Live them out. And build something that reflects *who you are*, not just what you do.

KEEP GROWING—SO YOU CAN HELP OTHERS GROW

At one point I did a review of my life. I looked at everything I was involved in—my business, my family, my schedule—and pared it all down. But once I did that, I had enough white space that I was bored!

It gave me space to find opportunities to further my goals, one of which is being a leader developing other leaders. So, I taught a leadership class for the American Institute of Architects (AIA) Leadership program, and while I was the Houston AIA president, I ran a book study for board members, using *The 21 Irrefutable Laws of Leadership* by John Maxwell. But I still had more to give, so when my daughter asked if I would volunteer for SPURS, a Girl Scout Leadership Program using horses, I had the time and was able to say YES!

You never know where the opportunities to share your leadership skills and help develop others will show up. Since then, my days are full but in the most fulfilling, empowered, and purposeful way. I'm not just growing a business. I'm growing *people*. Working with teenage girls is a gift and gives me so much hope for the future. And every time I show up, I remember that we're never done developing as a leader.

Today, I coach and mentor 174 girls and 50 adult volunteers in the SPURS program. I bring everything I've learned from the business world—DISC profiles, emotional intelligence, conflict resolution—and I use it to coach girls *and* adults alike. Leadership doesn't start in a boardroom. It starts wherever you are, with whoever's willing to learn.

Early on, I noticed one girl, Amy, who was running the arena for the troop riding session, which includes twelve horses, twelve riders, twelve SPURS leading horses, and six adults. As a high D, (dominant, confident, direct), she speaks with confidence and takes charge. She was giving clear directions and keeping everyone on task. But the adults weren't responding well. The feedback I received was that she was rude and disrespectful. I knew what was really going on. Amy wasn't being rude. She was commanding space, and her tone was misinterpreted. So, I coached both sides.

I asked the adults: "What does disrespectful mean to you?" I helped them understand they were applying a label while Amy was simply leading from her own personality type. To Amy I said: "Here's how you're being perceived. I know you're not trying to be disrespectful. But if you add a please or thank-you, if you smile while giving instruction, it changes the whole tone and how you are perceived." She took the feedback, made the shift, and came across as more approachable while still staying in her power. Then Amy surprised me. She started to advise other girls with similar challenges.

The adults struggle because growing means stepping outside your comfort zone and many resist change. The adults are learning how to support a girl learning to lead. Leadership requires the courage to practice the *next hard thing*. And sometimes the next hard thing is realizing that to grow, you must let go.

LETTING GO TO GROW

Letting go of control may be one of the hardest lessons for a leader to learn. As adults we often feel that we must maintain a certain level of control to ensure success, but here's the truth:

If you cling to control, you limit growth. It's a mistake I see leaders make all the time. They don't want to give up the power differential. They feel responsible for the outcome, so they take over or micromanage. But when you do that, you don't just rob someone of the opportunity to contribute, you rob them of the chance to *become*. If you want people to grow, you must let go.

Set the goal and then let someone else try it their way. It might not be perfect or at all how you would do it, but the goal isn't perfection, it's progress.

I have created a leadership team to help me run my company. I'm letting go of the control I've had. Each brings something different to the team. Why? Because they're wired differently. They process information differently. They lead from different strengths. And that's okay.

The hardest part for many adults is flexibility. We've been sold a lie somewhere along the way that success equals pressure. That pressure makes diamonds. That striving for 100% is the only way to prove your worth. But that mindset sabotages people. When people feel pressure to perform, they shrink, second-guess and stop taking risks. When you remove the pressure, people get creative, think better and begin to lead. So, ask yourself regularly: How much pressure am I putting on my team? And how much am I helping *relieve* it?

Recently, we completed a full rebrand and launched a new website. It was a big undertaking, and our goal was to launch in the first quarter of our 20th anniversary year. But then we took a breath and decided it would be just as fine to launch in the second quarter. There was no drama. No tension. Just steady progress. In my earlier "old-Alyse" years, I would have cranked up the urgency, believing that pressure equals productivity. But I've learned that pressure and deadlines are not the same thing.

Letting go of control doesn't mean letting go of excellence. It means trading the illusion of perfection for the reality of empowered people reaching their full potential. It's not easy, which is the final lesson I had to accept...

LEADERSHIP IS NOT EFFICIENT

Let me offer you a truth that may challenge everything you've been taught about success:

Leadership is not efficient. Leadership development is *definitely* not efficient. It's not quick. It's not a box you check after a weekend seminar. Real leadership takes time, repetition and *patience*. That's exactly why it's so rare.

We live in a fast-food culture that demands instant results. We want the promotion, the perfect team, the overnight transformation.

But leadership doesn't work that way. People, like seeds, need the right conditions to flourish.

Whether it's a child with a sharp tone or a team member who made a mistake, we can't expect immediate change. You don't flip a switch on someone's behavior. You *walk with them* through the process. You teach, model, and give them time to stretch into who they're becoming.

And that's the same grace you must extend to yourself.

It takes *courage* to lead in this way. It doesn't always feel productive. It asks more of you than just your skills. It asks for your humility, patience, and emotional intelligence. But make no mistake, this is the kind of leadership the world is starving for.

We live in the world we do because of the leaders we've had. And if we want a better world—better companies, better governments, better schools, better families—we need *better leaders*. Leaders who are developed, not just appointed. Leaders who model growth, not just power. And here's the final truth: You cannot develop others if you are unwilling to develop yourself.

So, keep going. Keep becoming the leader others want to follow. Because *your* growth will inspire *theirs* and that's how we change everything. One leader at a time. Starting with me and you.

About Alyse

"Be better today than I was yesterday." Alyse Makarewicz, AIA, applies this philosophy across all areas of her life—as a mother, an architect, a business owner, and a mentor.

She's the founder and president of AMB Architects, a boutique Houston firm known for its collaborative design process and employee-first culture. Under her leadership AMB has earned national and local recognition, including Best Places to Work awards from *Inc.* and the *Houston Business Journal*. In 2023, AIA Houston named AMB Firm of the Year—a reflection of the values-driven environment Alyse has shaped over nearly two decades.

After earning degrees in architecture and environmental design, Alyse spent eight years in traditional firms before starting her own. From the beginning she set out to build something different. She believed a successful firm could also be a supportive one. Today, AMB prioritizes work-life balance, professional development, and a culture of trust—where people are empowered to grow, not just perform. That foundation has helped AMB deliver thoughtful design solutions while building long-standing client relationships.

Alyse is a graduate of the Goldman Sachs 10,000 Small Business program and is a Certified DISC Consultant, a Ziglar Legacy Certified Trainer, and a Maxwell Leadership Certified Team Member. These tools allow her to lead and coach based on each individual's strengths and communication style. Her leadership style is rooted in self-awareness, emotional intelligence, and a belief that personal growth fuels professional excellence. She's committed to growing people, not just business.

Alyse volunteers her time to the AIA locally and nationally and has served as the Houston chapter president and on the national Small Firm Exchange board of directors, among other roles. She is a lifetime member of Girl Scouts and her daughter's troop co-leader. Together they mentor girls and adults through the SPURS equestrian program.

Alyse is just as active in her personal time, building massive LEGO projects, crocheting, reading, and traveling with family for energetic vacations such as hiking the Appalachian Trail. Her downtime often mirrors her work life: hands-on, intentional, and full of purpose.

Whether guiding a design team, mentoring a teenage girl, or leading a boardroom conversation, Alyse leads with clarity and intention. She believes good leaders don't cling to control—they create space for others to rise.

Her story is a reminder that leadership isn't a title. It's a daily choice to grow, listen, and help others do the same.

CHAPTER 10

YOU RISE

Leading Through the Storms of Change

By Cheri Perry

I didn't see it coming. Not the change. Not the grief. Not the unmaking of the life I thought was mine. My thirty-five-year marriage was essentially over, and to say I wasn't crushed would be a lie. I expected lots of seasons in my marriage—but not this. What happens when change doesn't knock? What happens when it just barges in, uninvited, flips your furniture, and tosses your carefully constructed life across the floor?

That was this moment. And while I would never have chosen it, I now know it was calling me into one of the most important transformations of my life. It was then, in the midst of internal chaos, I heard the question again—the one that had anchored me years before: What are you doing with the people God gave you?

I've always said, when change comes knocking—whether it's in business, a diagnosis, or a relationship—you don't run. You rise.

What I didn't realize then was that I'd been preparing for this level of change for decades. Every pivot, every personnel shift, every lost client had been giving me quiet training in navigating change with grace. Learning how to feel the feelings without retaliation. To respond, not react. I was developing the muscle of resilience, one decision at a time. Life is a continual classroom. Albert Einstein said it best "Once you stop learning, you start dying" so the better option, even in the midst of change, is to continue to learn!

My husband and I had co-founded Total Merchant Concepts and built it into a respected, nationwide financial services firm. I didn't want to give up on my marriage, on our business, or the life we'd built—but sometimes, change doesn't give you a vote. It just shows up and says: Let's see who you really are. That's what change does. It doesn't destroy. It reveals. And while the enemy comes to steal, kill, and destroy (John 10:10), I believe—now more than ever—that God uses even the most painful seasons to fulfill His plans for us (Jeremiah 29:11).

I've always been a student of personal development. I studied under Zig Ziglar himself. Suddenly, the books I'd read, the certificates on my wall, and the tools I'd taught were no longer theory. They were lifelines that came to confirm the answer to the question: Could I walk the talk?

That morning, I made a decision: I would not let this ending destroy me. I would look back at every moment when unexpected change cracked something open, only to reveal something better on the other side. I would go forward and call on every strength I have to ensure there was a positive outcome to even this situation. That's not to say there weren't heart wrenching moments, dark days or times when I felt like just pulling the covers over my head—but I was thankful for that focusing question.

THE QUESTION THAT CHANGED EVERYTHING

In 2012 I was sitting in a Ziglar Legacy class when Bob Beaudine asked me a question that landed like a thunderclap: "What are you doing with the people God gave you?" At the time, I was embarrassed by my answer. I had all the signs of external success—but I wasn't truly investing in the people I led. What a wake-up call!

From that day forward, I made a decision to live differently. To lead differently. To see people—whether in the checkout line or across the dinner table—as gifts and to treat them accordingly. That question permeated my life, so when the storm in my personal life broke, I found myself asking the question again, but with a twist: What am I doing with the people God gave me in this season? This time my answer was different and more powerful:

I was loving them. Focusing on my son. Leaning on my team. Choosing to see the positive in people despite the negative circumstances. Showing up for my friends and family. That question became my anchor, and it remains my anchor today. It's said that character is who you are when no one else is looking, and my focusing question revealed who I was and who I want to be. It also serves as a reminder that leadership is not about having it all together—it's about how you show up when everything's falling apart. It's about choosing the focus in the storm.

EXPECTING CHANGE

It's easy to brace for the storms we see coming—but what about the ones we should've anticipated and didn't?

I remember when my son Tyler left for college. I was fully prepared for the logistics: tuition payments, dorm shopping, flights home for holidays. But I wasn't prepared for the silence in our home. I wasn't prepared for the ache of a quiet kitchen table, or the shift in my identity as a mother. Those changes *should* have been predictable. But emotionally, they caught me off guard. That's the thing about change. Even when we expect it, we're often not ready for how it will *feel*.

Expecting change doesn't mean we become cynical or always wait for the other shoe to drop. It means we *live with wisdom*, knowing that nothing stays exactly the same forever. People evolve. Seasons shift. Businesses pivot. One of the earliest (and hardest) business lessons I learned came from a ten-year partnership with a major bank. We had no reason to suspect trouble, but one day they canceled our contract without warning. They had just sent in a new rep to "learn from us"—essentially having us train the person who would replace us. It felt like betrayal. I was furious and I responded poorly. I let anger lead. I didn't show up as the leader I wanted to be. Instead of learning from the loss initially, I focused on the loss and let the poor actions of others play a large part in how I responded, and it wasn't pretty! That loss stung—but it didn't sink us. In fact, it became a launching pad once I finally woke up and decided to lead rather than sulk. We rebuilt stronger. We diversified. We grew.

Losing that important relationship taught me to expect change—not with dread, but with wisdom. Change is not the exception. It is the rule, so don't be shocked when it shows up; instead, be ready and fully aware of the possibilities revealed by the change!

Here's what I've learned helps most when building a life that's ready for change both personally and professionally:

- **Build margin into your life.** Schedule room to breathe. Overloaded schedules collapse easily.

- **Keep short accounts.** Don't let unresolved conflict fester. Grace clears the runway for change.

- **Lead with flexibility, not fear.** Rigidity resists growth. Curiosity welcomes it.

- **Assume nothing is forever.** This is not pessimism—it's preparation. And it makes you cherish the present.

When you expect change, you can meet it—not as a threat—but as a teacher. And that teacher will shape a version of you that's wiser, more grounded, and more capable of leading others through their own storms.

Embracing Change

Embracing change doesn't mean pretending to love it. It means accepting it as the price of growth. It's proof that you're alive—and that something new is being asked of you. One of my hardest life lessons came when an employee I loved like family resigned unexpectedly. I'd been at his wedding. I assumed he'd be with us forever. But he couldn't see his future here—the vision I painted did not seem big enough for his goals and dreams. That experience reminded me: if your team can't see their future inside your vision, they will find another one. I thought I was being a good boss. But I had mistaken efficiency for relationship. That's management—not leadership.

Leadership is personal. It means choosing people, not just productivity. Not fitting them into your story—but helping them grow into their own. I often think of embracing change like stepping onto a moving escalator. It feels off-balance at first—your footing isn't sure, and you're not quite in control. But if you trust the movement and let it carry you, you'll eventually land on solid ground again—only this time, you're at a different level.

When I embraced the reality of my shifting life, I also saw my business through a new lens. Our culture became stronger, not weaker. My transparency during that season invited others to be honest about their own struggles. It built trust. Here are a few simple truths that help me stay grounded when embracing change:

- Let yourself grieve. It's okay to feel the loss before you grow from it.
- Ask better questions. Instead of "Why me?" ask "What now?" or "Who can I become through this?"
- Choose presence over perfection. People don't need you to have all the answers—they need to know you're still in it with them.

What I learned is this: embracing change doesn't weaken your leadership. It strengthens your humanity. And people don't follow perfect leaders—they follow present ones. The ones who show up, even when things are uncertain.

Employing Change

There's a difference between surviving change and employing it. Surviving is just making it through. Employing it means asking: What is this change or situation trying to teach me? How can I use this?

I've come to believe that employing change is a bit like enrolling in an unexpected course—no plan, no warning, just a syllabus handed to you in the form of a challenge. And whether we like it or not, we are in the class. The good news? We get to decide if we'll be passive observers or active students, and the cream always rises to the top. It's the same with change, we can rise above what we perceive as adversity and become better leaders. When we lost that bank contract, I started asking better questions:

- What was my part?
- Could I have served better?
- Were there warning signs?
- How do I make future partnerships stronger?
- How do I exit with grace if needed?

Those questions shaped my leadership. Today, we have more than two hundred referral partners. That one loss turned into a lesson that fueled a whole new era of growth.

When my son went off to college, I had to begin asking great questions and taking positive action. What is my purpose beyond being a Mommy? How can I fill this space with something wonderful? When my marriage ended, I had to do the same. I picked up the business pieces once handled by my husband—and discovered I was more capable than I'd given myself credit for.

Employing change means refusing to let hard things happen to you without requiring them to also work *for* you. It transforms wounds into wisdom and resistance into resilience. Here are a few signs you're employing change (not just enduring it):

- **You're learning, not looping.** You've stopped replaying the loss and started applying the lesson.
- **You're building forward, not backward.** You're not trying to get "back to normal"—you're creating something better.
- **You're grateful in the middle.** Not just when it's over, but while it's still messy, you're thanking God for what He's teaching you.

Change will ask more of you. But it also grows you. Don't just get through change. Employ it. Let it make you wiser. Stronger. *Braver.*

GRACE, GROWTH, AND THE PEOPLE GOD GAVE YOU

When I finally told our leadership team that my marriage had ended, I made them a promise: the business would keep running. I would keep leading. And I would not lead from a place of victimhood. Victimhood blocks growth. It dims the light of hope, and it disempowers the very people watching to see how you'll respond. A wise friend once said: "Judas ate too." Jesus knew Judas would betray him, yet He invited him to the table. Why? Because Judas' character didn't change Jesus' character. That principle guides my leadership: I can't control how others show up—but I can always choose how I show up.

Your Secret Weapon

That brings me to one extra tip—beyond *expecting, embracing* and *employing* change, there is one more critical thing you can do to help you navigate even the toughest of storms well. Leaning into your FAITH and having serious conversations with God when you are walking and working through storms, will provide the guidance you need. It might be through friends or through reading verses in the Bible, but you will find the solutions when you seek them with all your heart.

When I felt weak, I stood anyway. I led anyway, because people were counting on me, and because I needed to remember who I was. I leaned heavily into my relationship with my Heavenly Father and drew strength from Him and His word. Isaiah 40:31 says "But those who wait upon the Lord will renew their strength. They will soar on wings like eagles; they will run and not get weary; they will walk and are not faint." My friend Bob Beaudine wrote a book called Two Chairs (I highly recommend it!!) and he asked three questions that you might want to ask yourself:

- Does God know the situation?
- Is it *too big* for God?
- Does God have a plan for your life?

Spending time with your creator every day *is* your *secret weapon*! When I combine all of these tools and remember that winning in life is really all about relationships, I set myself up for success in this crazy world filled with all kinds of changes, both expected and *not*!

So now, whether in leadership, heartbreak, or growth, I return to that one question: "What am I doing with the people God gave me?" Because at the end of the day, leadership isn't about titles, it's about service. And the people in your life—right now—are not accidents. They are assignments. Expect Change. Embrace it. Employ it. Let every pivot, every painful moment, and every unexpected turn become training for your next breakthrough.

Change isn't the enemy. It's the divine curriculum for growth. And when you welcome it with courage, integrity, and a whole lot of heart—you don't just recover. You rise.

About Cheri

For nearly three decades, Cheri Perry has helped leaders, business owners, and teams grow stronger by aligning purpose, values, and daily action. As a speaker, coach, and certified Ziglar Legacy Trainer, she brings powerful clarity to leadership development, culture building, and navigating change with grace. Cheri is the cofounder of Total Merchant Concepts, a national provider of business growth and payment solutions, and a company widely recognized for its heart-led approach and integrity in an industry not known for either.

Whether coaching executives, training frontline teams, or speaking on stages across the country, Cheri inspires others to "rise through the storm" with resilience, gratitude, and bold authenticity. She's also the creator of Let's Share a SMILE, a national movement celebrating everyday excellence and human connection.

Cheri has been featured in local and national media, has coauthored multiple leadership books, and is the host of events and workshops designed to help people thrive during life's greatest transitions. When she's not speaking or mentoring, Cheri enjoys great music around a campfire, kayaking around the Pacific Northwest, road trips, and dreaming up her next adventure with a journal, a cozy blanket, and a great cup of coffee.

Learn more:

- CheriPerry.com
- TMCCoach.com
- GetTMC.com

"Change isn't the end of your story—it's the beginning of your rise."

CHAPTER 11

LABELS AREN'T LIMITS

Mastering Success When the System Writes You Off

By Kevin Babb

By the time I was seven, the world had already decided what I couldn't do.

The test results were indisputable. "Highly dyslexic," they said, like a sentence handed down. And just like that, my world was rerouted. My parents were pulled into IEP meetings, and I was thrown into remedial classes with other kids bearing labels the system was unprepared to support.

No one came right out and told me I couldn't succeed, but the implication was loud. I might be able to get a job, but a career? Not likely. I didn't really understand what was happening. I was just a kid, moving from one special ed classroom to another, my classmates and I relegated to the margins, no one expecting us to do much other than show up. By high school it was clear: I wasn't college-bound. Yet with that realization came a silver lining. The school tracked me into the occupational route, and I was given the chance to attend a trade program. Sophomore year I left campus for half the day to learn how to build things. I did a nine-week rotation learning plumbing, electrical, masonry and carpentry. I didn't feel behind anymore—I felt *alive!*

By junior year I focused fully on plumbing. I worked, learned, and got my hands dirty. At the end of that year, they sent me to the state plumbing competition. I placed second. My senior year I went all in—working full time for a plumbing company and getting school credit for it. That year, I went back and won first in the state. Then, I went on to *nationals* and placed third in the country out of forty-five top students. By the time I was twenty-one, I was licensed and fully certified.

Today, I'm the proud owner of Babb's Plumbing, one of the top plumbing companies in our region of South Carolina. I've built something that serves others, employs good people, and supports my beautiful wife and children. I wasn't successful *despite* my disability; I was successful *because* of it. Dyslexia didn't destroy my path; it *designed* it. It forced me to look beyond the standard route. It showed me the beauty of working with my hands and the value of skill, and led me to adapt, persist, and problem-solve. What others saw as a limitation turned out to be the very thing that led me to purpose, pride, and a life built with my own two hands.

In plumbing and in business, you don't always see the full picture until you dig deep.

Plumbing taught me that the messy work—the stuff nobody sees—is what keeps everything running. Business is the same. You've got to be willing to get under the surface, to build something that lasts.

LESSON 1: DIAGNOSE BEFORE YOU DIVE IN

Being dyslexic taught me to see the world differently. What used to feel like a disadvantage turned out to be one of my greatest tools—especially in plumbing and in business.

I didn't realize it was unique until I was in my early thirties, but while most people process information linearly, dyslexic minds often work spatially. We don't just see what's in front of us—we instinctively *see around it*. We can see things in a 3D model in our minds, mentally rotate objects, visualize systems behind walls, and imagine how things fit together before they're even in front of us. That ability has been a gift in my line of work. In plumbing, diagnosing a problem often means seeing what others can't— what's behind the wall, under the floor, deep in the system. You have to see the *whole picture* before you ever pick up a wrench. That same principle applies to business. We *diagnose before we act*.

A while back, calls weren't coming in, and we had to figure out why. We asked the hard questions. We poked around. We tried a marketing company that didn't deliver and learned quickly that a shiny website isn't the same as a strategy. We pivoted, found a team that aligned with our vision, and started seeing real leads come in. Good diagnostics isn't a one-time fix—it's a way of thinking. You solve one problem, and it usually uncovers another. Whether it's a leaky pipe or a leaking sales funnel, the process is the same: Get curious. Look deeper. Stay flexible. And never assume the first thing you find is the root of the issue. Sometimes success requires you to dig, pivot, and diagnose all over again. That's not dysfunction. That's growth!

LESSON 2: CHECK THE FLOW

In plumbing, if the water isn't flowing right, something's wrong in the system. Maybe it's a blockage or a leak, but one thing's for sure: You don't guess your way through it. You *check the flow* and trace the problem back to the source. The same goes for business.

Early on I'd have techs in the field make mistakes, and I'd catch myself asking, "Why did you do it that way?" And often the answer revealed a weak spot: "I didn't have a procedure to follow." That's when it clicked. If people don't know what's expected, it's not their failure; it's mine. When you want consistency in results, you need consistency in *process*.

We started documenting everything. Step-by-step procedures, video walk-throughs, troubleshooting guides, written and visual, handed out like tools in a toolbox. If a team member doesn't know how to handle something now, it's not because they weren't trained, it's because they didn't follow the system. And that's the beauty of good systems: They remove guesswork and reduce errors.

A business needs clearly defined operations to run smoothly. Otherwise you end up patching the same leaks over and over again. Having procedures in place isn't about control; it's about *empowerment*. It allows your team to move with confidence and keeps business flowing, even when you're not in the room.

LESSON 3: USE THE RIGHT TOOLS— AND USE THEM WELL

In plumbing—and in life—success doesn't always come down to brute force. It comes down to using the right tool for the job. I learned that early on, not just in the field but in the classroom, thanks to a man named Richard Bear. He was my teacher and mentor at the trade school, and he believed in us before we believed in ourselves. He also taught me the value of being resourceful.

Our trade program didn't have a big budget. What we had were donated materials, used equipment, and a teacher who knew how to stretch a dollar. When we were soldering pipes and the molten metal dripped onto the concrete, it would cool and peel off like foil. Every Friday, we'd scrape it up and sweep it clean, and someone would melt it down to make new solder sticks. We worked our way around a nonexistent budget. Even now, in business, I know there's always a way to make something work if you're willing to look at it differently.

Being dyslexic has forced me to live that way. I've always been a phonetic speller, which used to make writing invoices a challenge. Back when we used carbon copies, I'd scribble them out, and my wife, God bless her, would input them into the system, somehow deciphering my spelling like a code. I can only imagine what my customers thought they were reading. But I didn't give up. I found *tools* that worked for me. We moved to a cloud-based CRM that syncs on a tablet, spell-check included. It wasn't just about convenience. It was about *adapting* to the parts of my brain that operate differently.

Here's the truth: Your limitations only stay limitations if you refuse to get creative. The best plumbers don't use every tool— they use the *right* tool. And the best business owners don't try to force what doesn't work; they build systems that match how they're wired. Whether it's a soldering stick made from scraps or a CRM platform with autocorrect, success isn't about doing it like everyone else. It's about figuring out *how you do it best.*

LESSON 4: APPLY THE RIGHT KIND OF PRESSURE

In plumbing, pressure is everything. Too little, and nothing flows. Too much, and something's going to burst. The trick is knowing how much pressure to apply and when. Leadership is no different. Whether you're leading a team or leading yourself, it's about applying enough pressure to inspire movement—but not so much that you burn out or blow up. That balance is especially important when you've been conditioned to think you're at a disadvantage.

As someone who's dyslexic, I know what it feels like to be underestimated and to *internalize* those expectations. In my late twenties I had been working in fire service for six years. Because of my learning disability, I always had the option to have state exams read to me. It was part of the system and my IEP accommodations since I was a kid. And I used it. No one ever asked, "Do you think you could try it on your own?"

One day I decided to find out. I took the class, refused the assistance, and read the exam on my own. I was slow, but I passed, and at that moment, a switch flipped inside me. I'd been using my learning disability as a crutch—not intentionally but because I had let other people's limited views of me shape my own expectations. It wasn't until I took the training wheels off that I realized I could ride without them just fine.

Later, when I went for another plumbing certification, I faced that same internal battle. The test was computerized, nerve-racking, and I could've asked for help again. But I didn't. I challenged myself. It took me two tries, but I passed.

Leadership is not about ease; it's about *ownership*—of your process, your progress, and your pressure. As a leader in my company today, I practice that same mindset with my team. I don't expect perfection. I expect honesty, effort, and a willingness to grow. I apply pressure when it's needed and give space when it's earned. I encourage my team to find out what they're capable of, because the moment you stop letting other people define your limits is the moment you take charge of your own story and step into the life you were meant to live.

LESSON 5: MAINTAIN WITH METRICS AND MENTORS

In plumbing the work doesn't end when the pipes are installed. You have to maintain the system. Without maintenance even the best-built systems will break down. Business is the same way. I used to think the biggest hurdle would be *starting*. But it turns out, sustaining growth is the harder part.

I remember wanting a hydro-jetter—a serious investment for our company at the time. I thought I'd have to finance the entire thing and pray the money came later. But I did the math, tracked the numbers, and saved money while the machine was being built. By the time it was ready, I paid in full. That one purchase changed how I saw everything. I learned that in business, just like plumbing, you don't guess. You test, measure, and project so you can maintain your upward trajectory. *And* you find people who've already done it better than you. That's where mentorship comes in.

I started my business in 2007 after realizing I wasn't built to say, "Yes sir," to just anyone. But I also wasn't fully prepared for what business would demand of me. The phone didn't ring on its own. So I went back to the fire department working twenty-four/forty-eight-hour shifts and used those two off-days to build the business. I did that for eleven years, until 2019, when I finally left the fire service to go all in. That's when the *real* learning started.

We grew fast. We had trucks, equipment, and employees, but couldn't seem to break past $500,000 in annual sales. I reached out to Ellen Rohr, a franchising expert. She listened, asked the right questions, and gave me the truth straight: "You're not ready. But here's what to do instead." She gave me two books: *Where Did the Money Go?* and *The Bare Bones Weekend Biz Plan.* We started to see small improvements.

One day I got an email from a guy named Howard Partridge. I didn't recognize the name, but the email was an invitation to a business-owner boot camp in Texas being hosted by Partridge and featuring Rohr. I wanted to meet her, so I said to my wife, "Let's go. But we're *not* buying anything." We went…and bought *everything.* We joined the Inner Circle, and after about six months something clicked. We stopped surviving and started *strategizing.* We stopped reacting and started *measuring.* We shifted from hustle to ROI thinking. And with that mindset came growth. Today, we have a strong team: three field techs, my wife running operations, and a full-time CSR. The business is not just surviving—it's *flourishing.*

Maintenance doesn't just keep things running. It helps you scale. You maintain with measurements and mentors, because the right coach won't just give you tactics; they'll challenge your thinking. And when you find people who've been where you're going, it's not just support; it's a shortcut.

You're Not the Label—You're the Legacy

If you've ever been given a label—dyslexic, autistic, learning disability, different—I want you to know that the label does *not* define you. It might inform your experience. It might change how you navigate the world. But it does *not* determine how far you go, what you're capable of, or the kind of life you get to build.

I was labeled "highly dyslexic" at seven years old. They said I might not get a diploma. They never imagined I'd run a successful company, but here I am. Every pipe I've ever cut, every business risk I've ever taken, every problem I've ever diagnosed has been filtered through a brain that works differently. And that difference? It's been my *advantage,* not my anchor.

Today, I have a son who carries his own labels. And you know what I tell him? Your brain isn't broken. Your path isn't limited.

You don't have to fit someone else's mold to build a life you're proud of. Yes, our labels are part of our story; they don't *direct* the story. *You* do that.

So whether you're building a business, chasing a dream, or simply trying to figure out where you fit in this world—remember that you're not here to meet expectations; you're here to *exceed them*. And every tool, every challenge, every twist in the pipe? It's forming something stronger than anyone can see right now.

Your differences might shape the beginning of your story, but they have no power over its ending.

About Kevin

Kevin Babb is a master problem-solver, systems thinker, and legacy builder who has turned a childhood learning label into a lifelong advantage. Born and raised in Greer, South Carolina, Kevin graduated from Riverside High School before launching into a twenty-plus-year career in plumbing—where he quickly distinguished himself by competing and placing in statewide and national plumbing competitions.

Today, Kevin is the founder and president of Babb's Plumbing & Backflow Services, one of the most trusted and fastest-growing companies in the Upstate of South Carolina. A licensed mechanical contractor and DISC-Certified Human Behavior Expert, Kevin is known not just for his technical expertise but for his ability to lead, mentor, and diagnose problems—both in business and in life—with precision and purpose.

Before going full time in business, Kevin served seventeen years in the fire service, earning the rank of engineer and certification as an EMT. That experience, combined with his hands-on knowledge of plumbing systems, gave him a rare ability to lead under pressure and build systems that serve others with excellence.

Outside of work Kevin helps lead a men's group at LifeSong Church and is passionate about faith, family, and service. He enjoys camping, puzzles, and spending time with his wife, Heather; their two children, Wyatt and BellaJane; and their cockapoo-Westie, Sophie. He's also an unapologetic fan of LEGO bricks—because sometimes the best systems are still built one piece at a time.

Connect with Kevin:

Babbsplumbing.com
Info@babbsplumbingsc.com
864-303-6541

CHAPTER 12

BATTLEFIELD TO BOARDROOM

My Small-Business Fight for Survival

By Jim McDonough

The bullet tore through my flight helmet, sending shock waves through my body as I tried to keep my aircraft upright.

While fighting in Iraq, in the fall of 2006, my wingman and I were scanning every rooftop and alleyway for threats while providing area security for a route clearance team under constant attack while working to reduce a roadside bomb. The enemy wasn't aiming at our ground forces anymore. They traded up to a more valuable target, one that makes international news quickly. The insurgents were aiming to shoot down an aircraft. *That's when the shots arrived.*

I never saw it coming, just felt the violent impact as my helmet jerked sideways. Several bullets passed above my armored side panel; one passed straight through my helmet—and somehow missed my head entirely.

By every law of physics and every rule of probability, that round should have killed me. No broken skin. No visible wound. Just a concussion—and a story I still struggle to understand.

After years of processing and a good bit of therapy, I finally came to understand. This didn't happen *to* me. It happened *for* me.

ONE THING LEADS TO ANOTHER

My first eighteen years of service involved aviation life cycle management, encompassing everything from receiving the mission to threat analysis, mission planning, execution, and personnel recovery when things go sideways. Late in 2007, with my extensive career history and recent combat experience, I was recruited by the Aircraft Shoot Down Assessment Team (ASDAT), the Army's component of the Joint Combat Assessment Team (JCAT). Our role was to understand how threat weapons or their effect interacted with our aviation platforms, reduce these risks, and increase the aircrew and aircraft's survivability. We reverse-engineered many combat losses to gain the knowledge that would go on to save many lives. Our dead have one last story to tell. It turns out that the skills that kept helicopters in the air and soldiers alive on the ground are the same skills that make or break a business. As David Wright said, "Honor the process, and the process will honor you; dishonor the process, and the process will dishonor you."

When I retired from the Army in 2012, I thought I was trading multiple deployments and combat zones for the quiet world of small business. Instead, I found a different kind of fight—the small-business owner's battle for survival. Two years before I hung up my uniform, I envisioned building a service company that would give me more free time to chart my course, make a little money, and be my own boss. *Yeah, right!* I had a plan written on three bar napkins, a military retirement, and a battle buddy who would soon become my business partner. What could go wrong?

Veterans Cleaning Solutions LLC was started in my driveway, and we earned our first dollar in mid-2011. We entered the business world as technicians, not business owners. The initial successes were rewarding. We put money in the bank and purchased more equipment as we grew. We engaged a company to help us do market research and create a business plan. We were off to a good start. In the beginning it looked simple on paper. Provide carpet cleaning and lawn services to home and small-business owners across the Wiregrass region of Lower Alabama.

We began encountering more and bigger problems once we scaled past our fourth team member. We purchased additional production vehicles before we had a dedicated sales team. We had wide variations in consistency and volume of work. Our bank loan terms were crippling, and the payments on our debt were piling up. The business was on my mind 24-7; I had no real freedom; the business owned me instead of me owning it; I had very little family time, constant exhaustion, both mental and physical, and major stress; and I felt as if I was putting brush fires out most days. Can you relate to that? I needed to be strong and ask for help. In a society that views asking for help as a sign of weakness, we broke ranks.

We were introduced to the Alabama Small Business Development Center (ASBDC). The ASBDC helped us refresh our business plan, taught us the language of business finance, and laid out a debt-restructuring plan. The big game changer was when we hired two business coaches. We hired AC Lockyer with Softwash Systems® and joined Howard Partridge with Phenomenal Business Coaching. Hiring a business coach was our wisest business decision. Lockyer and his wife, Karen, came to our office and spoke reality into us. I didn't like what I was hearing, but I needed to listen. Partridge brought us the Simple Dimple Business Plan. This is a proven business system with the curriculum we needed to install into our failing business. We were asked to do two things: learn the systems and implement them. We were soldiers; we could follow directions. We implemented the Softwash Systems® 5 Star Company Business Model, and today, we are international instructors for that system.

Growth happens much faster when you can take a proven business system off the shelf, tailor it to your needs, and implement it on Monday. We went from running the business in my driveway during a pandemic in a town of twenty-eight thousand people to a dream team earning seven figures. Our dire situation began to change when *we* changed. With limited resources and unlimited options, we chose to follow *one system*. And it worked.

STEP 1: START WITH A PROVEN FRAMEWORK

"Leadership is the art of getting someone else to do something you want done because he/she wants to do it," according to Gen. Dwight Eisenhower.

John Maxwell said, "Everything rises and falls on leadership." And Dr. Robert Rohm said, "Leadership is an inside job."

Then I heard Howard Partridge say, "Leadership is effectively communicating your vision." No one can deliver consistent and high-quality results from a plan in my head. I needed an easy way to get the company's vision out of my head and onto paper, to provide direction for the team to accomplish our collective goals. As a small-business owner, I needed to plan the way I was trained to plan. You don't just set a goal; you chart a course.

We began using Partridge's Simple Dimple Business Plan in 2014. It is so simple that it is used in 120 different industries. Now called the Phenomenal Business Growth Planner (PBGP), we use this system for annual planning and quarterly "Way Ahead" meetings to keep us on track while maintaining a clear line of sight to our yearly goals.

Plan your flight; fly your plan. Writing a business plan was hard initially, even with professional assistance. Organizing and putting my thoughts on paper took me many weeks. Now with Partridge's PBGP, my staff does this in two hours every quarter without me. The leaders at our service company rarely need me around these days. They run the business day to day. With more free time I navigate other small-business owners through this exercise in about a weekend using the Phenomenal Business Growth Planner. I use the word *navigate* for a reason—it is not my company; it is theirs. Ellen Rohr said, "The simpler you make it, the further you can take it."

Step 2: Write and Follow a Written System

"What does the book say?" I love saying this because I would cringe whenever I heard, "Hey, Jim," right before someone would drop a problem in my lap. Today, with written systems, this rarely happens. Systems are a group of working parts that duplicate results consistently. A checklist is the simplest form of a written procedure. You either build your own or buy your business systems when you buy a franchise. Ask any of our team members at our service company, and they will show you their written procedures guide. We only get paid to do the work once, so we aim to do it right the first time. Systems take the pressure off the people. Those people are you, your team members, your subcontractors, and your clients. Systems are the basis for your training programs. How do you troubleshoot without a system?

Systems also protect profits and the employees' paychecks. In the military, taking the same ground twice is too costly in human capital; it consumes precious resources in business. I wasted so much time trying to get technicians and our sales teams to comply with the procedures in my head. It frustrated everyone. So, drawing back on my training, the simplest thing to do was document what I did every day and make it into a checklist. We built our checklists off national Deep Cleaning and Restoration Standards. There are fifty business systems common to every business. Did you know that? I didn't, and that was why we struggled so hard.

Step 3: Become a Better Leader

I had a lot of work to do in this area. I needed to build myself into a talent magnet that others would follow. Leadership is not making the plan, handing it to the team, and expecting them to execute it. The best leaders involve the team in the planning process and get their fingerprints on the plan.

People support what they help create. If I wanted people to

buy into my vision, I needed to involve them in the building of it. I had to get to know my people and help them connect their personal goals to the company vision. Getting their dreams on the table was hard. Most people have never had someone else ask about their dreams and goals. Understanding what people want, not just from their job but for their life, has become our strategic advantage. Hiring the dreamless and the goalless is a transactional business model. We are in the transportation business. Helping families get from where they are to where they want to go, using our framework is a transformational business model.

When team members see their goals embedded within the company's goals, we don't have to motivate them; they show up motivated. It's not just a leadership theory. It's a law of human nature. Zig Ziglar said it best: "You can have everything in life you want, if you will just help enough other people get what they want."

STEP 4: BUILD A DREAM TEAM THAT WILL RUN THE BUSINESS

"If you have a big dream, you must build up the team or give up the dream," according to Dave Anderson.

Hiring a team is only the beginning. Growing and retaining a team is the real work. We rarely fire people, not because we tolerate poor performance but because we invest in getting to know why they are the way they are. When someone struggles, we ask deeper questions:

- Is this a skills gap or a values gap?
- Is this a communication issue or a character issue?
- Can we coach them through this?

When you lead this way, misalignments solve themselves. I'll never forget what Dr. Robert Rohm, an authority on the DISC Model of Human Behavior, shared: "You can't change other people. However, a person can change themselves by learning to communicate better. You can learn to create deeper connections that change the world."

That one idea reshaped my view of leadership forever. It's not enough to manage people. You have to invest in them and connect with them. When you bring someone onto your team, you are hiring a human being, baggage and all. If you ignore that reality, you'll end up managing symptoms. If you embrace it, you can change lives. You do that by listening deeply, helping them understand where they are today, clarifying their dreams and their why, and building a clear pathway of growth.

At our service company, growth isn't optional. It's highly encouraged. Every team member is given the opportunity to develop through life assessments, coaching conversations, career paths, and performance reviews. Our most successful team members ask to be coached up.

Today, in a town of just twenty-eight thousand people, we run a seven-figure cleaning business because we develop people. Other businesses are asking us to teach them how we do this. Helping small businesses develop their human capital has become part of our calling: You don't grow a business; you grow people, and people grow the business.

After-Action Review and Lessons Learned

The best-laid plans, no matter how carefully crafted, are never guaranteed. No matter how much you prepare, the enemy always gets a vote. That's true in combat, in business, and in life. The real question is not whether you'll encounter resistance; it's how you'll respond when you do.

Most people call for help only after they are spiraling out of control. Strong leaders ask for help *before* they take flight. Plans fail for the lack of counsel, but with many advisers, they succeed. Having an adviser look over our plans before we execute is invaluable. A second set of eyes may see issues we are too close to. I share this story to advise you to seek assistance at the first signs of trouble, not as a last resort. I want this to increase your survivability and keep you from looking through the wreckage for forensic evidence. I've learned these lessons the hard way, so you don't have to.

I know what it's like to lead an organization into trouble—and to fight our way back out. And I know what it's like to sit at the intersection of opportunity and failure, realizing there will always be obstacles, and the only way forward is to grow faster than the obstacles around me.

Leadership is also an act of faith. You create a plan with the available time and team, formulate decisions on what you know, anticipate your most likely contingencies, and implement control measures to mitigate the risks. Then, you trust the process—that the work you've done is enough, that the people you've invested in will rise to navigate the challenges they'll encounter. The calling of one's life is not about perfection but one of perseverance. Smooth seas do not make a good sailor, nor do clear skies and calm winds make a good pilot.

I've carried that helmet with the bullet hole for years now, not as a trophy but as a reminder—a reminder that the line between life and death, success and failure, is razor-thin. Being shot at was a feature of my profession as an Army aviator assigned to the cavalry. You don't get to control when the shots come. You only get to decide what you do after. I'm still here for a reason, and my reason is simple: to help others lead better, aim higher, and fly further. Your business should serve your life—not consume it.

About Jim

Jim McDonough—Phenomenal Business Coach | Business Owner | Leader

Jim McDonough is a believer, devoted husband, proud father, seasoned business owner, and trusted Phenomenal Business Coach. He is the president of Phenomenal Business Coaching Inc. With a career grounded in discipline, leadership, and strategic execution, he brings a powerful blend of military precision and entrepreneurial grit to the world of small business.

As a retired US Army Aviation Combat Forensics Officer and Master Aviator, Jim served twenty-two years, including multiple combat deployments. That experience taught him how to lead under pressure, think critically, and adapt quickly—skills he now uses to help business owners break free from constant brush fires and take control of their companies.

Jim's coaching is rooted in a forensic approach: He doesn't just ask what's wrong—he helps you uncover *how you got here.* Having built a successful home service business, he understands the overwhelming nature, sleepless nights, and relentless pressure of running a business. He's walked that path and knows what it takes to scale to seven figures with clarity and confidence.

He has utilized programs from the Chamber of Commerce, the Small Business Development Center, and the Phenomenal Business Coaching System. Jim is living proof that the right combination of support, encouragement, and accountability can transform a business—and a life. His mission is simple: to help small-business owners stop being slaves to their businesses and turn them into predictable, profitable, turnkey operations that create true freedom.

Jim currently serves on the board of directors for the Alabama Small Business Development Center and mentors entrepreneurs through the Hudson-Alpha Navigate Program. He is an international phenomenal business coach, a mentor, and a speaker. He is committed to raising up the next generation of strong, purpose-driven business leaders.

If you're ready to regain control, build a dream team that runs the business for you, and scale with purpose, Jim is the coach who's been where you are and knows the way forward.

"Your business should serve your life—not consume it."
—JIM MCDONOUGH

Learn more: www.phenomenalbusinesscoaching.com/jim.